TOTEM ANIMALS

PLAIN & SIMPLE

TOTEM ANIMALS

PLAIN & SIMPLE

CELIA M. GUNN

THE ONLY BOOK YOU'LL EVER NEED

HAMPTON ROADS

Cover design by Jim Warner
Interior design by Kathryn Sky-Peck

Hampton Roads Publishing Company, Inc.
Charlottesville, VA 22906
Distributed by Red Wheel/Weiser, LLC
www.redwheelweiser.com

Sign up for our newsletter and special offers by going to
www.redwheelweiser.com/newsletter/

ISBN: 978-1-57174-748-8

Library of Congress Cataloging-in-Publication Data available upon request

Printed in Canada

MG

10 9 8 7 6 5 4 3 2 1

Contents

Introduction: What is a Totem Animal? 1

1   Totem Animals Around the World 5

2   Your Totem Animal 15

3   Working with Your Totem Animal 23

4   Strengthening Your Connection 31

5   Your Child's Totem Animal 37

6   Totem Animals A through Z 41

Conclusion 126

Index of Totem Animals 129

About the Author 132

Dedicated to Wolf, Crow, Buzzard, Blackbird,
Bee, Dragonfly and Owl, honored guides;
and to Anthony, Cindy, Grethe, Jane, Helen, Paul, Tipi,
Doug, Trish and Paul: true friends at a special time.

Ask the animals, and they will teach you; or the birds of the air, and they will tell you; or speak to the earth, and it will teach you; or let the fish of the sea inform you.

Job 12:7–8

What Is a Totem Animal?

Deeply ingrained in the tradition of North American Indians, who have protected the concept of totem animals to this day, the word "totem" is attributed to the Ojibwa tribe. According to the dictionary, a totem is an object, usually an animal or a plant, that serves as a revered ancestral emblem of a family or clan. Totem animals are used for personal guardianship as well; in this guise, however, totem animals are not passed down through the family or clan but are chosen individually.

To the Athabascan Indians of Canada, medicine is the art of connecting with a guardian or totem animal spirit. In the Athabascan tradition, this process is usually undertaken around the age of five years. The ritual is in the form of some sort of deprivation, such as a fasting quest, and the first image that comes to the child is the guardian spirit that will never leave. It might appear in the form of an animal, a bird, an insect, a reptile, a plant, or another spirit guise, and a bond is formed between the child and the guardian spirit that involves a certain interaction, with rights and duties. The totem is said to carry special influence over natural or magical forces, enhancing personal power, healing, and understanding. For the rest of his or her life, the child wears an item representing the guardian spirit: a piece of fur, a feather, a tooth, a symbol cut into wood. Without the guardian spirit it is believed that a person will die. While this first connection is of primary importance, other guardian spirits might be acquired throughout a lifetime.

Although the word "totem" is associated with North American Indians, the concept is found in some form in nearly all cultures. The idea of spirit guides speaking to and assisting humans through animals and birds is prevalent throughout the world. While some people might be more comfortable with the term "guardian angel" than with "spirit guide," others connect more strongly with the idea of animal energy. Many people, however, flatly dismiss the idea of having an animal or a bird as a personal spirit guide. "A fantasy; superstition," they might say. "We know better because science has told us that we are conscious, rational beings, and animals are not."

Yet, the idea that humans are superior to animals seems to have come at a great price. Having set ourselves apart from the natural kingdom, we have alienated ourselves from the very planet that we live upon. Having judged the instincts of animals as somehow inferior, we have come to distrust our own instincts. In so doing we have lost our own inner knowing, the knowing of intuition. Inner knowing is what helps us be truly creative and to make the leap beyond worry, fear, and pain; otherwise, we must make a rational decision about every step we take in life.

As well as helping you personally, coming to know and work with your totem animal will help you live in a harmonious relationship with the natural world and will link you to a long, rich tradition that connects us all to the sacred web of life.

Totem Animals Around the World

1

Long ago, our ancestors held all creation sacred. They understood that we are part of nature, that nature is part of us, and that we have an intimate relationship with the animals and plants with which we share the earth. Our ancestors drew no distinction between the natural and the supernatural, and the same holds for many indigenous cultures today. Reverence for the natural world is evident in most global traditions. Animals are beautifully and vividly portrayed in ancient cave paintings and petroglyphs all over the world, most famously in Lascaux and Chauvet, France. Sometimes people are portrayed as part animal; for example, a man with antlers. Many origin or creation myths tell of a time when the boundary between human and animal was thin, when an animal could become a human or a human could turn into an animal.

North American Indian creation stories describe animals and plants as the "First People." The First People jointly agreed to help humankind, whom they saw as weak and helpless beings, by sacrificing their lives to allow the humans to live. As part of this exchange, humans were endowed with the ability to communicate with the spirits of the plants and animals. According to these traditions, this capability brought Humans into the Order of Life.

It is believed that animal sounds are the origins of language, and many cultures have traditions that relate how animals taught us the skills we need for living. There are many tales of humans watching and learning from animal behavior. One of these tales explains that American Indians call the wolf "brother," since it was the wolf who taught them how to hunt. Native Americans understood that animals have wisdom to impart and can teach us; so to Native Americans, animals had status.

All over the world, ancient societies passed down legends, songs, and stories that prove the strong link that connects animals, gods or spirits, and humans. An inspiration to us all, they tell of a time when the spirits of animals communicated with humans, or the spirits or gods communicated with humans through animals. From Europe to Siberia, North America to China, this is part of a tradition that began during a magical time when humans were at peace with animals and when they understood each other's language.

Some ancient traditions named their tribes or clans after animals, birds, or fishes. The American Indians of the Pacific Northwest, for example, have a complex clan arrangement based on totem animals, represented by powerful woodcarvings, which closely associate them with the animals' symbolic power. Different traditions might have a tribal totem, another totem for the clan, and yet another for the family into which a person is born.

The Aborigines of Australia and the Bushmen of Africa have similar traditions of totems or power animals. Some Australian

Aborigine clans believe that the extinction of a species brings us a step closer to human extinction. The ancient Egyptians had some gods that were part animal, part human being. Ancient priests and priestesses might wear an animal skin to link them to the god and to the essence of the animal and to allow them to take on the quality or power related to the animal.

In ancient Greece, Aesop's fables for the most part portrayed animals, and their abundance of wisdom and foolishness. These stories have given rise to sayings still used today, such as, "cunning as a fox" and "wise as an owl." In ancient Rome, the augur studied nature and learned to read signs by observing the movement and behavior of birds and later of animals. Worldwide, fairy tales are full of animals speaking and acting powerfully.

Like the American Indians and Australian Aborigines, the early inhabitants of Britain revered the natural world, viewing rivers, forests, hills, and trees as the dwelling places of spirits. Ancient Irish, Welsh, and Scottish texts often tell of how the father of a hero is a god who shape-shifts into an animal or bird, who then visits a woman. The newborn child is then usually linked with an animal. Celtic clan names were connected to animals, and Celtic art is magnificently intertwined with animals and birds.

The Druids of the British Isles and northern Europe also had animal guides, and many are the tales of magicians having animals as familiars. Merlin is said to have taken a wolf as a companion when he retired. The British goddess Brighid is often depicted as a wolf, one of the guardians of Britain.

A pagan inheritance from pre-Christian times has carried over into early indigenous British Christianity (previously known as

Celtic Christianity) as a kind of nature mysticism. When monasteries were built over Druidic natural sacred sites, such as springs and groves, they were given the names of Christian saints and Christian rituals, but, reflecting a deep reverence for the land, believers celebrated God's creation, the natural world. Worship was often conducted outside under the heavens, in wooded areas or by a river. Brighid was Christianized as Saint Brigit, but was still depicted with a wolf by her side. Animals and birds were treated the same as human beings—with care, hospitality, and respect. Combining a

sense of spirituality with love for nature and all its creatures, people frequently told stories about saints who worshipped in wild and remote places and who had animals and birds as companions. Saint Columba of Iona honored a crane as a pilgrim guest. Saint Cuthbert of Lindisfarne communed with seals and sea otters, and spoke with birds.

Norse sagas tell of shape-shifting and familiars, while Norse and medieval heraldry picked up on the tradition of totem animals. Animals, birds, and plants were painted onto shields, banners, and headgear, tattooed onto people's skin, and carved onto settlement entrances. More than mere pictures, the totem animals acted as guardian spirits.

Contemporary Animal Tokens

The Lions Club, a worldwide volunteer organization, provides a contemporary example of how a totem animal might be unconsciously adopted. Sports teams in the United States often have animals as mascots. Christianity uses the fish and the lamb as symbols. Perhaps a child cuddles a teddy bear for comfort and believes that it helps, unwittingly but instinctively calling on the spirit of a totem animal.

Anyone who has read or seen the world-famous Harry Potter stories will not have missed the owl that acts as the young wizard's messenger. Although the concept is not fully explored in the stories, it appears that the owl somehow watches over the hero. Tradition tells us that the owl is associated with the teaching of magic, a perfect fit for a young wizard. Perhaps the reported surge in interest in having an owl as a pet that followed the success of the Harry Potter novels was because a number of people were taken by the idea of having that particular kind of familiar.

In the movie *The Golden Compass*, released globally in December 2007 and based on *Northern Lights* (the first book in Philip Pullman's *His Dark Materials* trilogy), each character in that alternate world has a helpful bird or animal daimon. This creature appears to be part of the person's soul, yet it expires when the person is killed, and the outcome for both when the daimon and the person are separated is tragic. Fascinatingly, in this version of the totem animal, the form of the daimon is flexible and changing throughout childhood and becomes fixed into one form only during adolescence.

The expression "a little bird told me" is still used today, although perhaps most often by older people. Implicit in this saying is that the information came in some secret or magical way that cannot be explained.

Shamanism

Sensing that chasing after "the new" is causing a split between themselves and nature, more and more people are being drawn to the "old ways." The oldest-known form of spiritual practice is shamanism. Most ancient societies throughout the world were originally shamanic and believed in animal allies and helpers; in other words, they believed that spiritual guides used totem animals to direct and empower human beings. Each community, tribe, or clan had its own shamanic way, learned through practice and experience. In modern societies, shamans are usually chosen for some notable quality and then trained, or becomes one because of some powerful event, such as a near-death experience. Also known among American Indians as medicine men (or women), shamans work with the otherworld to guide and assist people, as well as deepen their own knowledge and inner power.

Shamans believe there is spirit in all things. Working with ritual items made of clay, stone, or pieces of wood, or with skin, hide, feathers, or claws, in ritual or dance, shamans call on their totem animals. This is not an act of worship but an acknowledgment of the totem animals' power. With their help and protection, shamans can journey through their totems' elements—air if the totem is Eagle, for example, or water if the totem is Salmon—as well as in the otherworld. Shamans can call on the totem animals' help to empower their spiritual work for themselves and for their communities. Before a hunt, for example, contact is made with the spirit of the prey animal to explain the need for the animal's flesh and to give thanks for the creature's sacrifice. Shamans can call on their totem animals to access assistance from other spirit guides and indeed might have any number of totem animals to help them in their work.

Shamans can take on their totem animals' natural attributes, so the keen sight of Eagle would be reflected in clear vision, which might be physical but which is essentially spiritual. Taking on the guise of the creature by wearing skins or other animal or bird parts during a ritual or dance, shamans honor their animals so that they continue to ally themselves with the shamans and protect them.

This is such an important act that even today, in a competitive American Indian powwow, if some part of a dancer's ceremonial dress (also known as regalia, and representative of the dancer's totem animal) becomes detached and falls to the ground, tradition decrees that the dancer must immediately give away his or her whole outfit randomly to others who are watching. I saw this happen myself on a couple of occasions. This tradition is taken so seriously that there is a special ceremonial chant to accompany the dance of the four elders who retrieve the fallen item, even if the item is as small and seemingly simple a thing as a feather. The teaching is that the dancer has not given his totem animal enough respect, care, and attention, so there is some part of his spiritual walk that he or she has neglected. Then the dancer must work at putting new regalia together and, by doing so, attempt to learn what he or she overlooked. Finally, the totem animal's identity is usually held secret so that no other person can obtain power over it and therefore over the dancer.

You don't have to be a shaman to access or benefit from having a relationship with a totem animal, as everyone has access to a guiding spirit in his or her life. Animals behave in ways that can speak to us all, teaching us about the world and ourselves if we are open to watching and listening.

Your Totem Animal

2

When some people get to a certain level of spiritual evolution, they reach out and try to make contact with a totem animal. The way to do this varies according to different traditions and beliefs. For instance, some sources claim that the zodiac is the basis for totem animal teachings. In addition, there are different opinions about when we gain or obtain our totem animals, and whether we have only one animal throughout our lives or different animals at different times, perhaps obtaining a new totem animal on a temporary basis during a difficult transition in our lives. Still others believe that we always have a number of totem animals to call upon. As you become more accustomed to the concept and you access your totem animal and begin to familiarize yourself with it through practice and experience, you may find any of these ideas to be true. Don't feel that you have to live up to what anyone else says, because it is important for you to believe in the concepts that feel right to you and that work for you.

If you are just starting out on this path, it is preferable, I feel, to begin by making contact with only one totem animal; once you have established that relationship, you can branch out if you wish

and see what other totem animals want to be part of your life. Whichever way you choose, once you begin this journey, it will become obvious in some way when an animal or bird is trying to catch your attention or show itself in a special way. Keep in mind that all natural things communicate with us.

Think about the way your cat might stare at you so that you know it needs food, or even how your houseplant lets you know that it needs water.

The first thing to be aware of is that you don't simply choose your totem animal; it's more accurate to say that you choose each other. It is also important to keep in mind that spiritual guides work in their own way and time, not according to any human agenda. Essentially, the first lesson is that openness, willingness, and patience are all you need to connect with your totem animal.

As you attempt to make contact, you should not necessarily accept the first creature that presents itself, especially if it doesn't feel quite right. It is also essential that you recognize that you may have a hidden, inner desire to connect with a creature that is glamorous or powerful. Because many of us have lost our natural link to nature, the process might be compromised by this kind of wish. Remember that this connection is not about the power or the intelligence of the animal but about what the animal represents, and what is known as the *archetypal* power behind it that manifests through it, and how that power resonates with you personally.

Every animal has a unique essence and specialty, and it's important to remember that all forms of life have value and can teach us something. From a spiritual perspective, no animal is more powerful than another. The eagle symbolizes being close to the Creator because it soars high in the heavens and sees everything, while in the European tradition, the tiny wren is known as "King of the Birds," and legend says that it was the wren that brought fire to humankind.

Your relationship with your totem animal is unique and highly personal. Once your totem animal appears in your life, you make a

conscious choice to accept or reject it. Be aware that you are actually making a "soul agreement," so your finest relationship with a totem animal will be with the one that you feel is "right." Whether you want to share the knowledge of your totem animal with anyone else is entirely up to you. For some, it is a private relationship that is to be treated with the greatest respect and not lightly shared, lest its power become diminished or compromised.

The information about your totem animal may come to you because you have called out for it, as I did, or because you have set your intention and are quiet and receptive. It may appear in a totally unexpected way, although there are four recognized spiritual pathways to come to this kind of perception:

- If you have strong powers of visualization, you may use clairvoyance, or "clear seeing." Clairvoyance might actually allow you to see the creature, usually with your eyes closed but sometimes with your eyes open.

- Clairaudience, or "clear hearing," may enable you to hear the voice of your totem animal speaking inside your head, yet seeming to come from the outside. Be aware of a critical inner voice that may sound like a parent or teacher. Only accept the voice if what it says is helpful.

- A gut feeling and sense of your totem animal is known as clairsentience. It might come as a physical sensation or an emotional feeling, or a combination of the two, and it may be associated with an aroma or a scent.

- Finally, you may find your totem animal through insight or inspiration and just know that it is the one. This experience is known as claircognizance.

You may already be aware of where your greatest strength in these areas of acute perception lies, but if you are not, just spend a moment imagining your favorite place for a vacation. Is your immediate impression something you saw, a sound you heard, a smell you recall, or a thought about a place? Your need to find your primary spiritual pathway, although it is wise not to think you are limited to any one of them. To help you open up to your full potential, your totem animal may choose to appear through any of the others.

How to Find Your Totem Animal

To find your totem animal, settle yourself in a quiet place where you won't be disturbed. You may wish to light a white candle or burn some incense. Sit or lie down, close your eyes, take several deep breaths, and relax. Now you can begin the process of asking your totem animal to reveal itself. Remember, it is up to the totem animal to decide when to appear, but you must begin by asking, as that is the key: You have to make a deliberate attempt to ask. Ask politely, perhaps like this: "Please show yourself to me as soon as the time is right for us."

Then imagine yourself somewhere in the natural world. You might choose a favorite place, such as a lake, a forest, the mountains, or a desert. Stay relaxed yet alert; keep your mind open and receptive. Give it time. Let the creature come to you. You will know in your heart that the creature that appears is your totem animal. When it does and you are certain, thank it.

As the experience comes to a natural end, take your time to come back to everyday reality. Slowly begin to move your hands

and feet, legs and arms. Then open your eyes and look at your surroundings to ground yourself again. If nothing has happened, be patient. At the right time, your totem animal will appear. The important thing is that you have sent out a clear message. Soon there will be a clear response. Don't dismiss the experience; try again the following day or a few days later. Over the next several days, be alert for signs and coincidences. Your totem animal may appear in a way that somehow stands out, such as in a themed gift or in a dream.

Your relationship with your totem animal will not happen by chance. Its characteristics will somehow match your own personality. Remember, the key things always are respect and gratitude, for you and your totem animal are going to become a team.

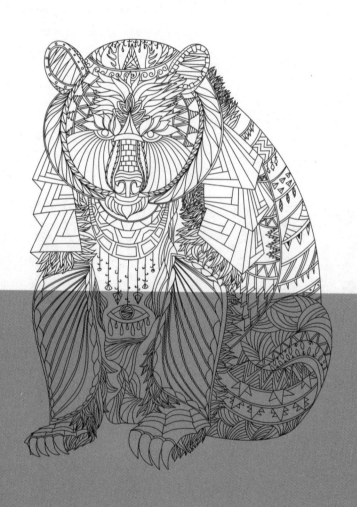

Working with Your Totem Animal

3

Once you have fully connected with your totem animal, you can learn how to work with it. You can ask your totem animal at any time for help and advice with questions or concerns you may have, such as when you are troubled or confronted with a difficult situation or have to make a tough decision. If you are going on a long journey, you may ask your totem animal for help and protection before you travel.

When you want to talk to your totem animal, you need to be in a quiet space where you feel comfortable and you won't be disturbed. Always make sure the telephone is off the hook or turned off. Sit or lie down, making sure your back is straight to minimize discomfort or cramp.

Honoring your totem animal as you approach it will always make the process easier. For example, if Swan is your totem, you might wish to demonstrate your respect by holding a swan's feather as you prepare to meet it. The medicine, or power, item will help you make the connection. Treat your feather or other item carefully by keeping it in a special place, and hold it mindfully, as this will also make a difference. Always respect and look after your medicine items. If you wish to help the process further, you can perform a small ritual such as lighting a white candle, burning incense, drumming, or chanting. This ritual can be done sometimes, every time, or not at all, as you prefer.

Starting the Journey

An effective way to begin the journey of communication with your totem animal is to start by imagining yourself inside a cave.

- Paint a picture of the cave in your mind's eye—dark and shadowy, perhaps with a little light coming from the entrance.

- Below and around you, visualize bare earth and rocks.

- Feel the roughness of them under your hands. Imagine cool air brushing your skin. Conjure up an aroma of damp earth.

- Take a moment to fully realize yourself within the cave. Then, when you feel it is the right thing to do, leave the cave.

- Go outside into the environment where you might naturally find your totem animal. This might be a misted forest; a steep, craggy mountainside; open, grassy plains; steel-blue, heaving ocean waters; spreading circles of ripples on a still lake; a dank, eerie swamp; or a sandy, windswept beach or desert. Perhaps you are among the trembling leaves of a tree.

- Notice whether the sky is wide open, clear, or cloudy; whether there is a breeze, a wind; whether there are scents such as crushed leaves or grass, damp earth or crushed pine needles.

- Take in the beauty.

Perhaps you wish to stay inside the cave, because this is the natural home of your totem animal. Make the environment as real as you can, and feel the peacefulness of nature. All is in harmony.

In these natural surroundings, whether inside the cave or out, let an image of your totem animal slowly take form. It might be walking, running, or flying toward you, wings outspread, or crawling up a blade of grass. It might sit and wait for your contact. Perhaps its shape is at first shadowy, and then its fur, hair, skin, or feathers come into focus.

Enjoy the beauty of its colors, its sleekness, liquid or ponderous movement, the obvious good health of the creature. Does it move gracefully, like a swan on the water, or race swiftly, like a lizard over sun-baked stone? Is it looking at you? Smile gently to yourself and allow your eyes to meet those of your animal. What color are

its eyes? What is their shape? Are they narrow or wide, fierce or soft? Is there any sound? Can you hear the beating of wings, a call, or a cry? Can you smell muskiness or a sharp scent?

With all your heart, thank your totem animal for coming to you. Thank it for all the ways it has helped you in the past, even when you were unaware of its presence. Then ask if there is anything that you can do for it. Always remember to do this, so that you show gratitude, appreciation, and consideration.

If you have something specific to ask your totem animal or if you want help, make your request gently and politely. Keep it simple. This might mean you have to go over your question a number of times in your head before you ask to make sure you are saying what you wish to say. Always be clear. If you have no particular issue, you might ask whether your totem animal has any message for you now.

You can ask your totem animal to appear in a specific way or at a particular meeting place and to give you some sign or message that will be unmistakable and easily understood. Over the following days, you will have to be watchful, pay attention to nature and to everything around you, and follow the signs as you are given them. A sign might come in the form of a gift, such as a book or picture, or in the shape of a cloud or in a dream. But it will be something that is beyond chance or mere coincidence, and you will know it when you come upon it. You may realize that you have been given a sign but the message is not very clear, so you may need to meditate on it or look up its significance in a book on symbolism.

Finally, when you feel that your communication is complete for this time, thank your totem again. Your gratitude demonstrates your appreciation of what you have been given, even if you don't know what it is yet. Remember that your totem animal always has your best interests at heart.

Come to the end of your journey by slowly returning to the place where you started, the cave, and with your eyes still closed, take several deep, cleansing breaths. Become aware of your body. Then let your eyes slowly open. Don't rush to get up, but reflect for a while on what you have just experienced; let it settle into your being like a leaf floating to the earth. You may wish to write your experience down, or record it, or make a note of it in some other way.

In the beginning, if you find it difficult to get in touch with your totem animal or if it seems like it does not want to come in response to your request, don't worry or give up in exasperation. This is a learning process, and it may be that, for the sake of your personal growth, you have to figure out what's going on for yourself. Your totem animal will appear at the right time; if that time is not now, then it will show itself when you try again later. The problem is not with you; the reason for the totem animal's non-appearance is never personal. It's important to remember that the concept of time as we know it doesn't exist in the spirit world.

You cannot own your totem animal any more than you actually own a pet, when you come to think about it. Coming to know and work with your totem animal takes practice and time. Be patient with the process and with yourself. The more you work with the process, the more you develop your knowledge of your totem animal and of yourself, your inner knowledge, and your spiritual understanding.

As you grow more experienced, you may wish to change the process of connecting with your totem animal to a routine you create yourself. Sometimes you may find all you need to do is focus your attention, breathe deeply a few times, and call upon it gently. You can then engage with it in a kind of conversation, in your mind or out loud, as you wish. Whatever method you do choose to use, always remember to thank your totem animal for connecting with you.

You are at the beginning of a wonderful journey that may change your life for the better and in ways you never imagined.

Strengthening Your Connection

4

Your connection with your totem animal is a dialogue of the highest spiritual order. Any ritual you perform when approaching your totem animal is a way of focusing your intent. If you feel comfortable with the idea, you might wish to refine your ritual further and dance as you drum, moving in the way that your totem animal would. This helps the spirit of the animal enter your experience.

Alternatively, you might sing or chant a sound you already know or something you make up on the spot. It can be quite simple and doesn't need to have any words. It can be as basic as a humming sound, or you might imitate the sound the animal makes. You can ask your totem animal to help you with this. Whatever you do, these actions will always help you when you call on your totem animal.

To further strengthen your connection, try to establish a closer relationship with nature by regularly going for a walk in a park, field, or woods, on a beach, or by a lake or river. Take along a pair of binoculars and learn to identify the birds that you see. You may eventually identify them by recognizing their song. You will see more wild animals than you might imagine, once you choose to become watchful. Take in the shape of the land, the undulation of hills and valleys, the sinuous curve of a river, the patterning of fields, the sharp jut of mountains, the contours of a lake, or the changeability of the seashore. Think about the environment in which you feel most comfortable. Do you prefer a feeling of openness and distance, such as you get from the sky, the horizon, or the open plains? Or do you prefer to pay attention to smaller details, such as the grass, pebbles, and stones under your feet? Do you prefer coast or inland, forest or open land, soft hills or rugged mountains? Your preferences will tell you something about yourself and perhaps also something about your totem animal.

Some American Indians call trees our "tall standing brothers and sisters," so as you walk around your neighborhood, learn to know them by the shape of their leaves, the appearance of their bark, and their differing patterns of leaf fall.

Depending on the time of year, you will be amazed by the variety of plants and flowers in your surroundings and the beauty of their blossoms. Try to learn about at least some of them. Many of them are actually "wild food," a concept that is becoming increasingly popular as people are trying to move away from processed foods. One of the best examples is the dandelion, which is a "weed" that grows in great profusion. When cooked, it contains more vitamins and minerals and is more easily digestible than spinach or chard. It is also a haven for beneficial insects such as ladybirds and butterflies. You will need to do some research before you begin to gather wild plants for your dining table or your medicine chest, but you will learn about your environment in the healthiest way possible.

If you are a gardener, you already have a deep awareness of nature and its cycles, but this can be enhanced by your attitude and mindfulness. Take the time to stop what you are doing, stretch your body, empty your mind, and look around you. Watch the birds that visit your garden. Do you know them and are you familiar with their songs? Observe the effect of the wind on your plants, and the rain, or the lack of it. Become aware of the differing responses of flowers on sunny or cloudy days. Find a comfortable place to sit and enjoy your garden, and as often as you can, empty your mind and let your garden speak to you. At night, before you fall asleep, mentally visit your garden and walk through it in your mind's eye, recalling the sounds of birdsong, of the wind. Most of the best ideas about how to arrange my own garden have come to me this way.

Note the differing places where the sun rises and sets over the course of the year. Watch for the phases of the moon and where it rises and sets. Take time to lie comfortably outside on a clear night and let your eyes explore the patterning of the stars. Do not worry about their names. Look for those very clear nights when the Milky Way is visible, and think about how your most distant ancestors looked up and viewed the very same sky.

Discover the local prevailing wind and notice how the trees have responded to its direction. Become aware of the differing quality of the winds, some bringing soft warmth and others bringing a memory of the cold places that they come from. Imagine the lands or seas that they might have crossed to reach you where you are now standing. See whether you can find out which wind tends to bring a storm, and learn to recognize the signs. Take the time to watch its approach and smell the promise of rain it carries. Let rain fall on your skin. Feel it, soft, caressing, and refreshing, or harsh and stinging; open your mouth and taste it. Study the shapes of clouds and how they ride across the sky.

Watch the pattern of the wind dancing over water, and see how it has a similar rippling and sweeping effect on growing crops and seeding grasses. Learn to pay special attention to appearances and sounds.

Sometimes it may feel like the wind is blowing from one direction but you can see a layer of clouds very high up moving in a different direction. This reminds you that the atmosphere has currents and eddies, just like the sea, and just like your life. Find out about the jet stream and the monumental effect it has on our weather.

The direction from which your totem animal appears also carries meaning—and be aware that "direction" means not only north, south, east, and west, but also the direction from which your animal appears in relation to you. Is the animal on your left or right, in front of or behind you? Find out what each direction symbolizes according to various cultures, and see which meanings resonate with you. Count the number of creatures that have caught your attention or the number of times one makes a sound. Numbers have meaning, and there are many books about numerology that can help you find the meaning in the numbers you observe. All these activities will help you become more sensitive to nature and learn how to be vigilant. You will also find you can get in touch with your totem animal more quickly this way. As you develop a greater respect for all life, you will find greater power, control, and peace in your own.

As you achieve a closer communication with your totem animal, keep in mind its qualities and characteristics. For example, is it hunter or prey? What can this tell you about yourself? Does it have a migratory pattern? Its natural habitat has a symbolic nature that can tell you something about yourself. For example, if your totem animal is most at home in the woods or a forest, do you feel the same? Use this information to come to know yourself better. The answers to these questions will somehow be a reflection of you.

All this is important practice for helping you speak to your totem animal. Becoming aware in this way will assist you in meditating outdoors and with asking your totem animal for signs, for help, and for communication. For a few minutes every day, close your eyes and let some of the things you are learning and experiencing settle in your mind. Meditating in this way will help you understand, especially as your experience begins to deepen and widen.

Your Child's Totem Animal

5

A child's imagination is unhampered by teenage and adult beliefs and prejudices, so young children are natural at this kind of thing. Helping your child find a totem animal, and perhaps involving your child in your own quest, could be a lot of fun, and it could bring you much closer to each other.

Before you share the idea of a totem animal with your child, think about whether your child ever pretends to be an animal, either indoors or outside in nature. Does he or she have little habits or reactions that remind you of an animal? Think about whether your child likes to draw a particular animal, or whether the child has mentioned that a certain animal keeps appearing in his or dreams. If you take your child to the zoo, does he or she have a special reaction to a certain animal?

However, even if you think you know your child's totem animal, be careful to find a good way to ask about it. Never try to guess; the first creature that your child comes up with often is the right one. If your child doesn't seem to know, don't tell him or her your idea of what it might be; instead, encourage your child to think about it until he or she comes up with the answer.

Knowing your child's totem animal will help you understand your child and learn how you can assist in his or her personal growth. The totem's characteristics will reflect the young person's self-expression, strengths, and weaknesses. This will help you see in what circumstances your child needs support and when your child is best left alone. Remember that your youngster must face challenges in order to grow and develop.

Several years ago, I taught a class in native studies to fourth-grade students at an elementary school in Canada. Out of the

thirty children in the class, I discovered that only two wished to be cowboys and the rest readily identified with the American Indians. At that age, most children are still naturally close to nature, and they have a deep respect for the land and its creatures, as well as a strong sense of harmony and justice; all of these qualities are traditionally attributed to the American Indian. Sadly, all these characteristics are being eroded by a general fear of allowing children to explore and play imaginatively and freely outdoors; caregivers are instead focusing children's time and attention on structured activities and the questionable values of television, computer games, and the Internet. Play activity is crucial to children's development.

There are a number of ways in which you can help your child find his or her totem animal, and the avenues to explore are similar to your own.

Totem Animals A through Z

6

Ant: self-sacrifice

Keywords: patience, effort, teamwork

The ant is a social insect, so it is a symbol of working for the community. It is a Celtic symbol of diligence, and in Jewish lore, it represents industriousness. In all cultures, the ant is viewed as a builder, able to carry up to fifty times its own weight.

As your totem animal, Ant teaches you how to manifest your dreams. An active person who likes to plan, you have the power to change not only your own life for the better, but the lives of others too. Understanding the power of the group, you perform well as part of a team and readily shoulder your share of the work. Ant helps you with patience and persistence, so you succeed where others might fail.

If Ant has just crossed your path in a special way, be aware of your efforts and opportunities in life. As the life span of some queen ants is twelve years, a specific period of activity (be it twelve weeks, months, or years) may be at hand. Perhaps you need to consider working with a group. Trust in natural law, and practice patience, so that harmony will flow. Remember that you always receive what you need "in time, on time."

Badger: willpower

Keywords: strength, protection, courage, earth, peaceful warrior

Associated in lore with the underworld, and a symbol of warrior energy, the badger is a very strong and brave animal that is built

for digging. Traditionally, the Scottish *sporran* (a pouch worn with a kilt) is made from badger skin as a symbol of protection. The badger set (or burrow) is highly organized and clean.

Badger is a powerful totem animal that reveals the secret, sacred energies of the land. It represents a grounded entity that is in contact with the power of the earth and its ability to sustain. With Badger as your ally, you can learn to understand the healing power of plants and roots. You understand that clean surroundings provide the principles for healthy living conditions. Having great strength of body, mind, and spirit, you can easily hold your own when faced with opposition.

If Badger has crossed your path, it may be saying that you need to retreat within yourself. Find a peaceful place in nature and draw power from being close to the earth. Do not blame others. Badger has appeared to help you discover your personal power and fight for your rights, to take control of your life and build what you want for yourself.

Bat: initiation

Keywords: perspective, clairvoyance, magic

The bat is a symbol of good luck and longevity in the Far East, and in Central America it symbolizes the rebirth of a shaman. Active at twilight, it is considered a doorway to other realms, so it is almost universally regarded as connected to the powers of the underworld. Viewing the world upside down, as it hangs in a cave or tunnel, the bat is also considered to represent transformation into a new clear-sightedness.

Interested in understanding the way of magic and of dreams, with Bat as your totem, you are helped in progressing through new levels of perception. Increasingly sensitive to where you are going, you are being removed from a state of illusion. The path of the magician is full of lessons about seeing, and Bat symbolizes the true clarity of inner sight, of looking at things from a completely new perspective by turning things on their head.

If Bat has flitted around your head in the darkening twilight, you are being guided to look within yourself and find what you are wasting your time on or what is holding you back. It may be an old hurt or fear that needs to be brought to light so you can clear it away. Negative thought patterns stop you from developing, so a change of attitude may be necessary. Bat helps you look at things from a different viewpoint and helps you know when to make a move.

Bear: self-sufficiency

Keywords: introspection, ancient wisdom, self-confidence, discrimination

Many societies throughout the world believe the bear to be the ancestor of humans. Honored for more than ten thousand years, this totem has inspired the naming of the two constellations that revolve around the polestar: Ursa Major and Ursa Minor. Able to hear over great distances and to remember the smallest hurt, the bear is considered to have great powers. According to northern European tradition, it is king of the animals.

As your totem, Bear teaches strength from within. Understanding that the answer to every question lies within, you prefer not to rely on others but to go within yourself for what you need to know and also to find the inner strength to do what you need to do and to stand up for what you believe in. Finding time to meditate or simply be quietly on your own is important to you, as it gives you the inner space to hatch new ideas and creative endeavors. Your judgment is usually sound and invariably respected.

If Bear has just lumbered into your life, it may be time to sit alone for a while and think about what you are undertaking or what you are going through. Perhaps you are confused and look-ing for answers from other people rather than paying attention to your own feelings and understanding. Bear appears to remind you that it is in the stillness within that all true knowledge begins, and to give you the extra strength to make sure and steady progress.

Beaver: achievement

Keywords: self-assurance; determination; productiveness; loyalty

Adapted for life in the water and on the land, the beaver repre-sents the realms of emotions and dreams. It mates for life, and its family is close-knit.

With Beaver as your totem, you always have something to do, not because you are afraid to stop but because you are a creative person who needs to be "as busy as a beaver." You rarely take on more than you can manage, so you also know how to take it easy and spend time with your family and friends. Reliable, loyal, and

good at teamwork, you can often come up with alternate ways of doing things, and that is when you tend to take charge.

If Beaver has recently appeared to you in a special way, you may have been feeling blocked in some project or relationship. Beaver will help you generate the enthusiasm to push yourself to act, or to open new doors to opportunity. Remember that there are many routes to manifesting your dreams.

Bee: creativity and mystery

Keywords: **divine inspiration, hard work, sweetness of life, rebirth, wisdom**

Throughout the world, the bee carries a breadth of symbolism ranging from resurrection to divine inspiration, wisdom, prosperity, and creativity. It was a symbol of royalty in ancient Egypt, and in ancient Greece, it was given the name of "the Great Goddess." Mead, made from honey, was believed by the Celts to be the drink of immortality, while the hexagonal shape of the honeycomb is regarded as mystical geometry. Also an emblem of Christ and the Holy Spirit in Christian traditions, in some societies the bee is regarded as the symbol of the sun and of the heart.

With Bee as your totem, you know where you are going. Capable of great creativity and frequently inspired to new endeavors for the good of all, you often achieve the seemingly impossible. When all else around you seems to have failed, Bee helps you draw strength from a deep reserve. Remember to take the time to enjoy your activities.

If Bee has just buzzed into your life in a special way, take note. You are entering a period of creativity that will require hard work. This may involve bringing inspiration or order into your life or into the lives of others. Bee reminds you to keep your focus and plan accordingly.

Bison: spiritual abundance

Keywords: prayer, synchronicity, giveaway, gratitude

The bison, or North American buffalo, is a symbol of spirituality and prosperity to the Plains Indians. The tale of White Buffalo Woman teaches the right kind of relationship between the material and spiritual realms and shows that, with sincere prayer and right attitude, whatever you need is readily available.

With Bison as your totem, you are a strong individual who understands personal responsibility. You readily shoulder your own burdens and try to use your spiritual and material energies for the highest purpose and the greatest good. You may face an occasional test, but your path in life is fairly straightforward. Bison helps you understand the principle of abundance, so you are always willing to share what you have, and you readily count your blessings.

If Bison has come to you in a vision, you are being helped to keep yourself grounded while walking toward a time of greater abundance. If things seem like they are a bit of a struggle, remember to have faith. Do not push the situation, but join right action with sincere prayers, and the path will open easily before you. Know that you are always provided for, see the good in others, and remember to be grateful.

Blackbird: new beginning

Keywords: magic, nature, initiation, ancient secrets, mysticism

The blackbird was one of the five oldest creatures of Celtic lore, and Celtic tradition tells how the blackbird led the way on the journey of initiation. As well as heralding spring, its enchanting song was said to be a means of travelling to the underworld, to access the hidden secrets of the goddess. Its beak was said to be yellow because it had dipped it in the treasures of the underworld. Associated with the blacksmith, who has a reputation as a magician who hammers out the work of creation, the blackbird was also a common familiar of witches and Druids.

As your totem, Blackbird inspires you to spend a lot of time outside, sitting quietly beneath a canopy of trees or by water. This helps you with new ideas and enhances your creativity, which you may find is often best expressed in late spring or summer. You are comfortable being alone and are fiercely protective of your space and your family.

If Blackbird has caught your attention in a special way, you are being called upon to make a journey to the underworld and to the womb of the goddess, as the first part of a new direction in your life. Spend time outdoors, listening to the beautiful song of the blackbird, as it can carry you between the realms. New inspiration is coming to you, as is a new connection to nature.

Boar: honor

Keywords: **courage, truthfulness, spiritual authority**

Courageous and daring, the boar used to freely roam the forests of Britain, Europe, and Scandinavia. A symbol of great antiquity connected with midwinter rites, it represents honor, truthfulness, and fertility. It was one of the most powerful totem animals of the Celts, and it was connected with magic and prophecy. The

position of swineherd was honored, and swineherds were often also magicians.

Boar is a powerful and protective ally that can teach you about the mystery of transformation. You have great personal integrity, a strong will, and a deep interest in hidden knowledge, which Boar can help you access and use wisely.

Boar appears when you are faced with a challenge in life. Perhaps you are feeling overwhelmed by a problem. Be brave, strong, and honest with yourself and others. Boar helps you take heart. Nothing is as bad as you imagine, so approach the problem directly, and fear and worry will dissipate.

Bull: determination

Keywords: strength, foresight, patience, passion

Almost all Mediterranean and Middle Eastern traditions had a form of bull worship, and the bull was the symbol of regeneration and fertility all around the world. In early versions of the zodiac, Taurus the Bull was the first sign of the zodiac. The Druids believed that the bull represented the sun. A white bull was the totem of the Druid seer as he embarked on a vision quest to dream of the rightful king.

Often a totem of a king or high priest, Bull teaches of the reliability and single-minded determination a leader needs. With Bull as your totem, you are strong and sure of yourself, yet able to sacrifice your own needs for the good of all. Well-grounded, you have great energy. Since the bull's horns represent a connection to the heavens and the moon, Bull can also help you with prophecy.

If Bull has just appeared to you in a special way, it may be that you need to prepare yourself for some hard work related to a present endeavor. Be patient and practical. Take a close look at the situation and make sure you are not being stubborn about some aspect of it. Perhaps you need to bring some passion to it; if so, Bull can help you with this.

Butterfly: transformation

Keywords: inspiration, courage, visionary, joy, color, dance

Since antiquity, the butterfly has been considered all over the world a symbol of the soul that cannot be destroyed by physical death. In medieval times, it was associated with fairies and elves, and in illustrations, these creatures were often given the colorful wings of the butterfly. The five-stage life cycle of the butterfly is an extraordinary representation of the stages of growth, whether of an idea, an endeavor, or a relationship.

If Butterfly is your totem, you understand that life is a colorful dance of joy that should not be taken too seriously. You accept that personal change is a vital, never-ending cycle and part of your growth as a human being. You know where you are in life and tend not to worry about what lies ahead, as you are fully present in the moment. A creature of the air, the butterfly is associated with the power of thought. The ability to know your own mind and to change it is your most powerful tool in growing through the many changes that life inevitably brings. As you are always ready to make changes, you are open to them when they come, as they inevitably must. You may like to wear colorful clothing and to dance.

If Butterfly has flitted into your vision, think about what is confronting you at the moment. If you feel stuck, perhaps you need to change your attitude. It could be that you are getting ahead of yourself. Maybe you need look at things differently or lighten up, or know that this is time for a change. See if you can identify what part of the cycle you are at, so that you can take courage and figure out what you need to do next. You may wish to find some private time to dance to music that really moves you or to join a dance class. You can discover much about yourself through dance. Take special note of the colors of the butterfly, as these may be relevant. For example, red denotes taking action.

Cat: mystery

Keywords: magic, independence, healing, clairvoyance, curiosity

In ancient Egypt, the domestic cat reached the most revered status, sacred to Bast, the goddess of healing and fertility and protector of the home, and also to her aspect as Sekhmet, goddess of destruction. In the Hindu tradition, Shakti, goddess of childbirth, rides a cat. The Celts believed that the cat had prophetic powers and that if you looked into its eyes, you looked into the otherworld. It was the totem animal of a Pictish tribe in Scotland, whose

land is now known as Caithness, "cat country." Known in folklore and fairy tales worldwide as a creature of the night, the cat is associated with the moon, the feminine, and the power of transformation.

Not an easy totem to call upon, Cat reflects your independent nature. A freethinker, you often do not behave as people expect. You sometimes take risks, but with Cat as your ally, you seem to live a charmed life. Naturally graceful and very sensitive, you are a curious and clever soul. Once you know what you want, you do not hesitate. You are interested in developing your psychic abilities and perhaps practice some aspect of the healing arts.

If Cat has crossed your path, look out for new magic coming into your life. Pay attention to signs and synchronicities so that you can act when the time is right. Follow your instincts rather than listening to others. If you face confrontation, know that Cat has appeared to protect you.

Cougar: leadership

Keywords: decisiveness, clarity, strength, personal responsibility, grace

Also known as the mountain lion or puma, the cougar is a fast and efficient hunter. Stealthy, graceful, and agile, it also tires quickly.

Not an easy totem, Cougar helps you work through the many trials and challenges in your life, teaching you how to be calm and assertive but also how to stretch yourself and make swift and sure decisions. This can result in a tendency to take charge of a situation, which might make you a target for other people's criticism or resentment. Since you are very sensitive, their reaction may make you lash out sometimes, although for the most part you have control over yourself. Cougar teaches the responsibility that comes with power, and the knowledge that you are setting an example. You also know better than to insist that others follow your lead. You know never to take more than you need, and you can balance your power with extraordinary gentleness.

If Cougar has crept into your dreams or visions, it may be time to learn about your personal power. Perhaps you have been given a new responsibility and you now need self-confidence. Check your motivation and set your purpose clearly. Cougar will help you balance the energy of mind, body, and spirit. Don't hesitate, but take courage, follow your heart, and keep yourself focused. Remember, a mistake is only a mistake when it is repeated.

Coyote: paradox

Keywords: wisdom, foolishness, magic, simplicity, trust

Keenly intelligent and adaptive, the coyote has a rich tradition in North American lore. As creator and trickster-teacher, this totem is often associated with magic. Somewhat weirdly, this can represent magic that doesn't always work. This is because the coyote represents the balance of foolishness and wisdom, much like the jester in the medieval court, the Fool in tarot, and Loki of the

Norse myths. Playful, fun loving, and lazy, the coyote often forgets to learn from its own mistakes, but it is a survivor who always comes back to learn something new.

A difficult totem, Coyote helps you as you move from one challenging experience to another. With a childlike innocence and trust in the world, and a child's true wisdom, you do the best you can, and even if everything seems to be going wrong, you have faith that eventually things will work out and you will understand the hidden lesson. With Coyote as your ally, you have an instinct about the secret of life, which you understand is full of paradox. This helps you see the funny side of things and enables you to help others see the humor in a difficult situation. Needing mental stimulation, you adapt well to new situations and readily view things from a new perspective.

If Coyote has just loped into your life, it could be that you are bored with your situation or are facing a challenge. Coyote can help you with an imminent decision, such as whether you are likely to make a clever or stupid choice. Look for the positive in the challenging experience. Coyote comes, laughing, to teach you about yourself. Even if it is pained laughter, there is a deep and powerful lesson. Be honest with yourself; perhaps you are taking things too seriously or making them too complicated. Remember to take time off to relax and play.

Crane: regeneration

Keywords: focus, inspiration, knowledge, discrimination

In China and Japan, the crane signifies long life. In many societies, its mating dance was regarded as a magical ritual. The ancient Greeks and Romans copied the crane's movements and made them into a dance of power and regeneration that they performed

at the death of the old year and the beginning of the new. The crane also represented a labyrinth. The Celts regarded the crane as sacred to the king of the underworld, where lay the secrets of regeneration. A Druid possessed a crane-skin bag, which was the magical link to the secrets of the Ogham alphabet, a medieval alphabet used for the Old Irish language. In those times, writing was believed to call into manifestation whatever the written character represented.

With Crane as your totem, you prefer to focus on one thing at a time, but you can juggle if you have to. Crane is often the totem of the bard or poet, so you can readily access divine inspiration and bring your creativity into manifestation. Knowledge is important to you, and you like to pass it on. You have the ability to help make things clearer to others, as much as to yourself.

If Crane has just appeared in your life, it may be that you are being helped to recover some part of your emotional self. Look carefully at the way you conduct yourself. You may know a lot, but it is worthwhile sharing only when it is appreciated. If you are unsure about an issue, it may be helpful to walk a labyrinth with a question in mind; Crane will help you find the answer.

Crow: sacred law

Keywords: ingenuity, magic, prophecy, inspiration

One of the most intelligent of all birds, the crow occupies a prominent place in ancient traditions, folklore, and mysticism worldwide. The sacred texts of some North American tribes are under the protection of the crow. In Celtic tradition, the crow is the guardian of the gap between this world and the next. In many cultures, it is viewed as the master shape-shifter and is associated with witchcraft and prophecy. Wary but sociable, the crow utilizes a complex language, and it keeps a very clean nest.

With Crow as your totem, you have a high sense of personal integrity, and you understand and honor the higher order of harmony and balance. People often turn to you for advice. You watch for the presence of magic in the world every day, which helps you sense change that is coming to your life and to make any necessary adjustments. Crow helps you see things as they really are, understand the differences between human and spiritual law, and understand that our perception of the material world and the spiritual world is an illusion. There is an infinity of worlds.

If Crow has called for your attention, change is about to happen in your life. You may be struck by inspiration, or an opportunity to create something new and important may present itself. Crow is telling you not to hold on to the past. Take care to be honest, especially with yourself, so you can access your inner truth and know how to conduct yourself and speak up if necessary.

Deer: gentleness

Keywords: compassion, grace, intuition, hidden strength

In legends throughout Europe, the deer leads the hunter into the wilderness or forest, where the hunter obtains new teachings. In these stories, the deer is representative of the hunter's soul or higher aspect and of the need for the hunter to free him- or herself. Highly adaptive, deer are found all over the world, and they may have been one of the most important animals for the early survival of humankind.

As a totem animal, Deer may appear weak, but it is important to remember the great strength that lies at the heart of gentleness. If Deer is your totem, you are a private person, gentle in speech and touch. Sensitive to danger, you are acutely aware of what is best for you and those around you, and you can usually hear what truly lies behind others' words. You are non-critical, though, and you know instinctively when to push and when to allow. You willingly sacrifice your own needs for the sake of helping others.

If Deer has tiptoed into your vision, you are being reminded to listen to your intuition and to proceed gently. Perhaps you are contemplating change or need to resolve a situation; Deer reminds you to take the feelings of others into consideration. Be warm and careful rather than forceful. Perhaps you need to be watchful in a new situation. Take heart: Deer can ease your fears by inspiring you with heightened instincts and new insights. You are on your way to becoming your true self.

Dog: loyalty

Keywords: unconditional love, watchfulness, companionship

Descended from the wolf, the dog is the oldest domesticated animal. Connected to both solar and lunar deities, it has a complex symbolism and is often associated with death. In ancient Egypt, the jackal-headed god Anubis was a mediator between life and death, while dogs or dog-headed gods are also guardians at the gates of holy places. In Africa, traditional belief says that it was the dog that brought fire to humankind. A shaman may wear a dog's skin when performing divination. In the Celtic tradition, to compare a warrior to a dog was a great honor that was subverted only with the coming of Christianity. The strong spirit of the dog is not easily broken; it will still display love toward even a cruel owner who bends its nature to his or her own needs.

With Dog as your totem, you are intelligent, loving and loyal, and devoted to your family. You enjoy social occasions. Eager to help, you may be a healer, or you may be adept at counselling. Each breed has a unique function, but some are mixed, so it is important to contemplate the relevance of the breed. For example, if you have a hunting type of dog in mind, it may be that its free-ranging, independent spirit is reflected in you.

If Dog has appeared to you in a special way, perhaps you need to look at your approach to life. Dog is reminding you to live by your personal truth and to be true to yourself, your family, and your friends. Perhaps you need to look after yourself more and take time out to relax or play. Maybe you have been giving too much of yourself and you now need to set boundaries. Dog can help you with confidence in all these areas.

Dolphin: compassion

Keywords: breath, sound, play, communication, harmony

The ancient Greeks and Romans regarded the dolphin as sacred to many gods. The dolphin is honored worldwide, and sailors consider it a good omen. The French successor to the throne was called the "Dauphin," and the dolphin was part of the royal coat of arms. Inquisitive and quick to learn, the dolphin has always been

interested in humans, and there are many tales of dolphins saving people's lives.

Dolphin is the totem of an intelligent and creative person who readily takes on new projects. Taking life as it comes, you enjoy living in the present, and your delight in the world affects others strongly. Not competitive, you believe there should be no winners or losers but that everyone should have fun. Compassionate, highly intuitive, and deeply sensitive, you can often finish the sentences of those close to you. Naturally helpful, you fit well into a group. You have a strong focus and are serious about practicing meditation, during which you can readily access divine energy.

When Dolphin has swum into the sea of your life, consider the ebb and flow of creativity within you. If you are feeling blocked or stressed, Dolphin may suggest that you learn techniques of conscious breathing, as these can help release tension and revitalize your body. Practicing toning can assist with healing body, mind, and spirit and bringing your ideas into manifestation. Perhaps you need to take life less seriously. Think of Dolphin's "smile." Life is meant to be happy and free.

Dove: serenity

Keywords: spirit, peace, love

A ground feeder with the softest of songs, the dove traditionally has been associated with a great wealth of symbolism, especially with the feminine. It represents the purest and most powerful force a person can experience—love. Love transcends the physical realm, raises the spirit, and develops the soul. In Christian traditions, the Holy Spirit descended on Jesus in the shape of a dove while he was being baptized.

Having Dove as your totem brings many challenges. You may become a healer, as you have been deeply wounded at some point in your life. Lifted beyond attachment to material desires and possessions by the gentle power of Dove, you are dedicated to walking a spiritual path and content to do it alone, as it is a highly personal journey to you. People often comment that they feel a sense of peace enter the room with you. You are open to discovering how to receive love as well as give it, you are non-judgmental of yourself and others, and you do not wish to control people.

When Dove shows up in your life, you may be feeling upset about your path in life, as though you've lost your way. This "dark night of the soul" is a challenge for you to seek meaning. Examine the purity of your motivation, suspend judgment, and consider other perspectives. Dove has appeared to help bring peace and balance to your world.

Dragonfly: power of light

Keywords: transcendence, transformation, clarity, sensitivity, nature

The dragonfly has lived on the planet for more than a million years. An American Indian myth tells how the dragonfly was actually once the dragon, which eventually got "too big for its boots" and so was transformed into the dragonfly. Born in water as a nymph, the dragonfly dances in the realm of air as it matures, its wings reflecting and refracting light in a kaleidoscope of rainbow colors, like a prism. It can fly at high speed, hover in one place, and even fly backward.

If you have Dragonfly as your totem, you are deeply aware of how people (yourself included) can live under illusion, and you have the ability to part the veil and cast light on most situations. You may have suffered some deep childhood emotional trauma. Emotionally intense in your early years, with Dragonfly's assistance you have learned balance through mental clarity and control. A strong connection with nature is vital to you, so you must be outdoors in nature for part of every day. Often the totem animal of the gardener, Dragonfly is a messenger from the realm of nature spirits, devas, fairies, and the little people, and you can work with these beings if your mind is open to them. Our allies in the world of nature, they can help bring back balance in the plant kingdom.

Dragonfly appears when you need to see what is happening in a situation or relationship. Perhaps you are being too rational about an emotional matter, or maybe you are emotionally shut down or resisting change. It may be that you are busy with too many different things. Use your imagination to shed light on the situation. Ask Dragonfly to help you with a new perspective. Let color come into your life; try wearing colorful clothes for a change.

Eagle: spirit

Keywords: spiritual knowledge, fearlessness, perception, illumination

Prevalent throughout the world as a mystical symbol of sun and sky, the eagle is also associated with thunder and lightning. An icon of royalty since ancient times, the eagle was the ensign of Roman legions. To the Celts, it was the symbol of ancient spiritual knowledge. In Christian churches, the lectern for reading the Bible is usually adorned with the form of an eagle with wings outspread. All over the world, eagle feathers are used as sacred ceremonial tools.

Air is the main element of Eagle; it represents the realm of the higher mind and inspiration. The totem of an evolved spirit, Eagle helps you be both in and above the world. Adept at seeing the big picture, you are learning to work with all aspects of spiritual life and to reach new heights. Although this may mean you have to go through many trials and challenges, you understand that there is always a higher purpose than might be apparent at the time.

You have an excellent sense of timing, as you can see the past, present, and future. With such strength, however, you must be careful not to hurt others.

If Eagle has appeared in your life, it will inspire you with strength and insight that you can apply when finding a new opportunity. This may be in the form of a test that gives you great responsibility for your spiritual growth. It could be that you are too caught up in the details of your life or that you have become too opinionated, and Eagle is telling you to open up to new horizons and to view the larger perspective. If you are being faced with difficult choices, Eagle can assist you to rise above the material and to make the decision that is for the best of all.

Elephant: resolve

Keywords: knowledge, responsibility, confidence

Traditionally, kings rode this ancient and majestic lord of the plains and the jungle. In India and Tibet, the elephant is depicted as holding the world, and even the universe, upon its back. In Africa, it represents long life, great strength, and wisdom. The elephant clan is matriarchal, and the whole clan will rally to the defense of the young when needed. An elephant can find water when none seems to exist and can survive on the thorniest of vegetation. It is an animal of great intelligence, and nothing can stand in its way.

If Elephant is your totem, your heart is open and your feet are on the ground. You are intelligent, and you love finding out about new things and adding to your store of knowledge. You have great depth of emotion and a natural grace and humility. Resourceful and good at taking responsibility, you find satisfaction in being of service, whether to yourself, to your family, to the community, or in the voluntary sector.

Elephant comes into your experience when you know what you need but something seems to be in the way. The obstacle may be other people or it may be your own fears and doubts. Elephant can give you the strength to pull yourself out of unbalanced negative emotional states and the confidence to begin a new venture or relationship.

Elk: stamina

Keywords: perseverance, consideration, sister- and brotherhood

The elk is a powerful animal that can outrun most of its predators, and it is sacred to many North American tribes. Its thick fur can withstand extreme cold. It tends to keep company only with members of the same sex, except during the mating season.

With Elk as your totem, you are a wise person, comfortable in your own skin. Throughout your life, Elk helps you make steady headway, using your strength, energy, and abilities to the fullest while not overextending yourself. As you come to understand yourself, you willingly teach what you have learned to others. Enjoying company, you like to be with members of the same sex as much as with those of the opposite sex. If you are a parent, you are very protective of your children. You may be a vegetarian or at least include many vegetables in your diet.

When Elk shows up in your life, consider the way that you are conducting yourself. It may be that you are embarking upon a new project that really suits you. Elk has appeared to help you to pace yourself so you aren't burned out and can manage to see things through to completion. It might be a good time to work in a group situation for a while, gaining support and feedback, or to spend more time with others. If you feel that you lack energy, consider a vegetarian diet, even temporarily, because it may help raise your energy levels.

Fox: guile

Keywords: magic, cunning, feminine energies, decisiveness, adaptability

A symbol of magic, slyness, and cunning, the fox is respected all over the world. Seen as a shape-shifter in ancient China, it was viewed as a trickster in ancient Greece and in many European cultures. A talented animal, the fox hunts like a cat, lying in ambush and then suddenly pouncing. It also has a trickster charm, seeming to leap about crazily until its prey is so mesmerized by the strange antics that it has not realized it has allowed the fox to come too close. Adaptable, the fox is able to live in a town as readily as in the countryside, where it appears on the borders of woodlands and open fields, mostly at twilight and dawn. Both place and time represent the boundaries between worlds.

If you have had a difficult childhood, you may have Fox as your totem. This has taught you to be a private person who moves silently and watchfully and who blends into the background in any place or company. In this way, you see and learn things that others might never notice. Because you have developed a high degree of discrimination, you know when to avoid trouble and you are often a step ahead of everyone else. Comfortable with yourself, you can work in harmony with a group, where your contribution is creative.

If Fox has suddenly looked you in the eye, it has appeared to teach you about acting in a subtle manner and following your instincts. Perhaps you need to withdraw. It's possible that someone is not being truthful or is trying to trick you. Watch people's actions rather than listening to what they are saying. Pay attention to your intuition, trust yourself, and keep silent about what you are learning.

Frog: renewal

Keywords: **healing, purification, abundance**

In Japan, the frog is said to bring good luck. In ancient Egypt, it was associated with Heket, the goddess of childbirth and long life, and it was also a symbol of resurrection. Native Americans believe that the frog calls the rains that cleanse the earth. All over the world, the frog is associated with the moon and with creation.

With Frog as your totem, you are an empathetic person, very sensitive to the emotions of others. You know how give support without becoming entangled. As a symbol of metamorphosis, Frog helps you through many changes in your life on your way to coming into your own power, which is strongly creative and often connected with healing or with clearing negative energy from buildings.

If Frog has hopped into your vision, you may need to cleanse some area of your life. If you have taken on the emotional baggage of others, an effective way to clear it is to place both hands in a prayer position above your head as you breathe in, then pull your hands down in front of your body as you breathe out, finally pushing them outward from your solar plexus with a loud "pah!" If you are feeling bogged down or in the grip of negative thoughts or feelings, toning or chanting can help in releasing energy. Tears may be helpful. You may be awakening to a new power in your life. Take a break in your routine to allow this, try taking a long, hot soak in the bath, or visit some hot springs.

Giraffe: foresight

Keywords: insight, grace, sociability

A graceful, calm animal, the giraffe has keen eyes, and because of its long neck, it can see great distances. Highly protective of its young, the giraffe can move swiftly when it needs to. On its head are three strange skin-covered nubs that are not really horns. One of these is directly above the eyes at the site of the third eye.

If Giraffe is your totem, you don't waste energy by worrying; you look ahead with calmness and confidence, and you can often see the outcome of thought, word, and deed. Farsightedness and insight come to you in ideas, dreams, or visions. Committed to harmony and justice, you move forward through your life with grace and purpose.

If Giraffe has come to you in a special way, you know what you want but you need some assistance in moving forward. If you are worried, ask Giraffe to help clear away what is holding you back so you can reach for something new in your life. Don't be afraid to ask others for help.

Goat: perspective

Keywords: balance, support, sexual energy

Seen in India as the primeval mother, the goat is connected to fertility cults all over the world. Sacred to the Greek god of the sky, Zeus, the goat is also connected to Pan, the god of nature. The goat is associated with fairies, witches, and the wildwood, but was demonized by Christianity. Sure-footed and strong, it climbs easily and is very agile.

Consider whether your totem is a domestic or mountain goat, as they have slightly different traits. Both imply that you are ready to take risks and that you will always land safely on your feet, for you can see what you're getting into and you know how to behave. A free spirit, you need to follow your dreams and make your own rules. You are creative in many areas and can receive inspiration out of the blue, at any time.

If Goat has leapt into your life, it encourages you to believe in yourself. Perhaps you need support in a new endeavor. Goat reminds you to take the time to look ahead and then get on with whatever it is. Remember to make space to play and have fun too.

Grasshopper: extraordinary leaps forward

Keywords: courage, intuition, progress

Holding a position of honor in many cultures around the world, the grasshopper was a symbol of nobility in ancient Greece and of good fortune in China. Moving by leaping and hopping, it has the extraordinary ability to leap up to twenty times its own body length, which is how it escapes its predators. It cannot leap backward, only forward or sideways.

If your totem is Grasshopper, you are not the sort of person to progress in a steady way. Instead, you appear to sit still, then suddenly shock everyone, including yourself, by taking a great leap forward. Your intuition guides you as to when to make a move. Always trust your inner voice because only then will your jump forward into a new venture be successful.

If Grasshopper has hopped into your life, you are about to make a leap forward. You may not be aware of this, or you may be aware but nervous about it because it is so new. You are learning to trust and follow your instincts. Be attentive to possibilities and be ready to move.

Hare: creativity

Keywords: **watchfulness, agility, sensitivity, divination**

In mythology, belief, and folklore all over the world, the hare is associated with the oldest of deities, the Earth Mother. The hare was considered a lunar creature in ancient Egypt, India, China, and Mexico, and the patterns in the full moon were supposed to resemble a hare. In North and South America, the hare is a cultural hero. Sacred to the Celts and Anglo Saxons, who forbade the eating of its flesh, the hare was believed to hold ancient secrets about the renewal of the mystery of life through death. Their annual ritual hare hunt, dedicated to the Teutonic goddess Eostre, is the basis of the present-day Easter bunny tradition. Active at dawn and twilight, and during both day and night, the hare is seen to pass through all the realms with ease.

Hare is the powerful totem of an extremely sensitive and creative person. If Hare is your totem animal, you have a quick and fertile mind, and while your ideas may seem wild to others, they are actually new and inspired. You like to plan ahead and to use common sense, yet since you are flexible and able to move quickly when you need to, your endeavors are usually successful. A solitary person for the most part, you are well able to look after yourself. Under Hare's influence, you are interested in divination, the development of clairvoyance, and practices that fall under the influence of the moon.

If Hare has leapt into your life, a time calling for great creative energy is ahead. You are being guided to liberate your imagination, which will help see you through a predicament or seize a new opportunity. Perhaps it is time to break away from rules and boundaries that you might have set or that others might try to impose on you. Hare may be telling you to attune to the cycle of the moon. If you are a woman, honor your moon time and take note of how its cycle affects you so you can better understand your creative power.

Hawk/falcon: spiritual perception

Keywords: foresight, perspective, healing, strength

In cultures all over the world, the hawk represents the light that illuminates darkness. Sacred to the ancient Greek sun god, Apollo, because of its keen eyesight it was linked with prophecy. In ancient Egypt, it was sacred to the sun god, Ra, and its hovering stillness was linked to a fixed star in the heavens. Many cultures use a hawk feather in healing rituals.

Hawk is the powerful totem of a person who is a born leader. If Hawk is your totem animal, you have probably experienced powerful dreams and visions since you were a child. An extremely spiritual perspective allows you to readily access higher levels of consciousness, yet you have an eye for detail. As your judgment

is clear, you often take the initiative. Other people often don't understand you, your ideas, or your actions, but no one can tell you how to think or behave.

When Hawk catches your attention, be aware that a powerful message is coming. New powers, such as visionary abilities, may be about to be awakened in you. Perhaps you doubt yourself, or you need to stand back from a situation or relationship and look at it in a different light. Maybe emotions have clouded your vision or your plans have not worked out, and you need to take time out to look them over and go with the flow. Hawk helps you to see things from a new perspective and to balance your energy.

Hedgehog: self-knowledge

Keywords: true self, healing, self-defense

Prominent in Irish mythology as well as Asian and ancient Egyptian lore, the hedgehog was viewed as a wise adviser to humans. It was also connected to the invention of agriculture and to solar energy. In Europe, the hedgehog was thought to be able to predict changes in the weather. A solitary creature, mainly active at night, it protects itself by rolling into a ball so that its spiny coat acts as a defense. In winter, it semi hibernates, emerging from its shelter only on warmer days.

As your totem animal, Hedgehog helps you come to know yourself. You have learned to trust your inner voice and are comfortable being alone, and your inner life is so rich that loneliness is never an issue. Nor are you afraid of your shadow side, having come to understand that it is part of a necessary balance in life. An interest in the healing arts comes naturally to you, and you may find this to be your true vocation. You aren't the sort of person who seeks out trouble, but when it finds you, you can take care of yourself.

If Hedgehog has come to you in a special way, it may be that you need to set boundaries. Perhaps you are putting up with something unnecessary, or perhaps someone close to you is overly demanding; Hedgehog can help you defend your personal space. You may need to look after your health, so ensure that you get enough rest and eat well. Take a step back and look carefully at your life. Your intuition will show you what you need to know.

Heron: hidden wisdom

Keywords: vigilance, independence, balance, ancient knowledge

In ancient Egypt, the heron was a symbol of the solar cycle and of contemplation. In both Africa and Europe, it represented vigilance and divine knowledge. It stands watchfully in water, its feet anchored in the mud, but it nests high in trees, moving gracefully among the elements, symbolic of emotions, body, and mind.

With Heron as your totem, you are probably unconventional. Traditional roles do not appeal to you, so you see yourself as unique, with your own path to follow. Your intuition is strong, and the opinions of others are of little interest to you unless they have information that resonates deeply with you. A balanced person, you have your own way of doing things, and you are adept at seeing and seizing opportunities.

If Heron has appeared to you in a special way, you are being reminded that all answers, all wisdom, come from within. Perhaps you have been swayed too much by what others have to say or you have become too reliant on someone else. Heron can assist you with finding your own way through life, through being observant and listening to the teacher within you: your intuition.

Horse: mobility

Keywords: strength, divination, loyalty, compassion, power, speed

Represented in prehistoric glyphs in caves all over the world, the horse has a rich tradition in lore and mythology. In many traditions, horses pull the chariots of both sun gods and moon goddesses. The horse was also connected to burial rites and is considered sensitive to spirits. To the Celts, the horse was associated with the wind. Today, crests of waves are known as white horses, possibly through a connection to Neptune and his sea horses. The Saxons considered it taboo to eat horseflesh. A horseshoe is believed to be lucky, as it represents the lunar tradition.

As a totem animal, Horse helps you rise above the mundane and see things from a higher spiritual perspective. Your intuition is finely tuned, and you use reason to serve your intuition. Although self-contained, you are sensitive to others and you think before you speak. A compassionate, friendly person, you know that freedom of mind, spirit, and body is earned. You tend to look on life as a grand adventure.

If Horse has just shown up in your life, perhaps you are in rut and need to travel, to broaden your horizons, or simply free yourself from an unhealthy relationship or situation. Assert your freedom. Moving in a new direction will help you recognize your own power.

Kangaroo: balance

Keywords: detachment, simplicity, gentleness

Primarily a herd animal, the kangaroo inhabits massive areas of terrain. It can survive on scant amounts of any kind of vegetation during times of drought. Its massively powerful tail is used for balance and for self-defense. It cannot move backward.

With Kangaroo as your totem, you are not attached to past events or behavior patterns because you understand that you did the best you could at the time. To you, a "mistake" is a step forward. Balanced, able to live comfortably in the present, you believe that all you need will somehow be provided. You like to be with your family, and you usually put family members first. You also enjoy a lively social circle, but as you get older, you may increasingly prefer your own company.

Kangaroo appears as your totem when you feel that something is missing in your life. Perhaps you are caught up in a negative emotional or behavioral pattern or are in an unbalanced relationship or work situation. Kangaroo can help you move forward or find a place of balance. You might simply need more confidence. Remember to appreciate what you have, to let life unfold, and not to push things too hard.

Kingfisher: prosperity

Keywords: courage, intuition, the subconscious

In Greek myth, the kingfisher is a symbol of faithfulness, peace, and prosperity. One myth says that the kingfisher was originally dull gray in color, but when Noah released it from the ark it took on the iridescent colors of sky, water, and earth. In many cultures, it is a symbol of royalty. In European legend, the Fisher King is the keeper of the Holy Grail and the source of infinite wisdom.

With Kingfisher as your totem, you are a loving and giving person. Although it may seem risky to others, you are always ready to dive into new situations because the energy of Kingfisher helps you emerge with the best results. You have the ability to see what others cannot.

If Kingfisher has flashed into your vision, there is a new potential for abundance in your life, on either the material or spiritual level, and it may involve a seeming risk. Kingfisher can help you manifest the best outcome, perhaps by fishing something out of your unconscious mind.

Lion: dignity

Keywords: authority, wisdom, patience, family

From ancient Egypt, Assyria, Babylon, and Africa to China, Japan, India, and Europe, the noble king of the beasts, with its obvious power, golden yellow color, and mane like the rays of the sun, was commonly associated with the sun and with gold. As a symbolic guardian, the image of the lion can be found on thrones and in palaces and temples. Christ was known as the "Lion of Judah," and the same title was once given to the king of Ethiopia. The lion appears on heraldry and coats of arms.

Lion is the totem animal of a centered person who is loving but also assertive. If Lion is your totem animal, you are a natural leader

who is better in a group than alone. You have a certain presence, so people notice you when you come into a room. You are sure of yourself, and you know how to follow your heart. You are aware of your purpose in life, so you have the courage to be yourself. Not afraid of risk, you nevertheless weigh things carefully before you get involved. You avoid unnecessary conflict and danger, but you can take care of yourself. You are not afraid to speak up (or even roar) when you feel that it is needed. Family is important to you, so you enjoy being a parent, and you are a model of cooperation, affection, and patience.

If Lion has padded into your life, you may be about to face the challenge of a new lesson about your role and your authority within a group or community. You will be called upon to stretch yourself, to use your imagination and be creative, perhaps to speak up in a way that is new to you. If other people try to take your power from you, Lion will help you find the strength and wisdom to listen to your heart, so you can move forward with confidence, knowing you are fully protected.

Lizard: ancient knowledge

Keywords: dreamtime, divination, renewal

Throughout the world, the lizard is connected with the symbolism of light and the sun, which represent knowledge. In Native American lore, the lizard is associated with dreams. The part of our brain known as "the reptilian brain" is said to connect us with ancient prehistory. An extremely quick-moving creature, the lizard regularly sheds its skin. It can also lose its tail to foil a predator, and then regenerate it. All lizards have a residual third eye.

If Lizard is your totem, you have a vital life force. Extremely sensitive spiritually, physically, emotionally, and mentally, you are strongly psychic and intuitive. Lizard assists you with seeing into the unknown and acting quickly when you need to. Dreams are very important to you. You also possess an element of detachment that saves you from becoming too dependent on anything in your life.

When you need to explore new levels of perception, most likely Lizard will skitter across your path. Lizard is reminding you to meditate and to pay attention to your dreams. Maybe now is the time to start a dream journal. Certainly, you are being told to pay attention with all your senses and to learn to trust yourself. Perhaps it is time to let go of something that is no good for you anymore.

Magpie: metaphysical knowledge

Keywords: intelligence, balance, curiosity

Associated in many traditions with witchcraft, augury (the reading of omens), and the divine trickster, in China the magpie is an omen of great good luck. A large, distinctive bird, highly intelligent and inquisitive, it has a reputation for stealing shiny trinkets. Social yet cautious, the magpie builds a large nest in a tree fork, which is considered a place between the worlds. Alternatively, it nests in a thorn-bush, which also has magical connotations.

If Magpie is your animal totem, you are an unusual person with a powerful will. Interested in many things, you have wide-ranging knowledge and sharp intelligence. The metaphysical realms are of particular interest to you, and you can read and readily apply signs and omens to daily life. Aware that the quick or easy answers are not always the correct or best ones, you use your intuition responsibly.

When Magpie presents itself in a raucous or flashy manner, be aware that you may need to use your fine mind to advance yourself in work or in life. Take responsibility and get on with things rather than just talking about them. Perhaps you are looking for superficial or quick answers instead of applying yourself properly. Magpie can help you balance your practical side with your dreamy side.

Monkey: agility

Keywords: **balance, intelligence, humor, curiosity, creativity**

A complex and contradictory symbol worldwide, in the Far East the monkey represents wisdom and detachment from material things. The Three Wise Monkeys of Jingoro who "see no evil, hear no evil, speak no evil" represent the key to the right way to live. The monkey also reflects the actions of the unconscious mind,

jumping from one thing to another and acting on instinct. In fact, there is a Buddhist meditation method in which learning control of the mind is called "training the monkey." Thought to be the cleverest animal in the jungle, the monkey is seen all over the world as a magician who masks its great powers of insight and intelligence by clowning around.

A powerful totem, Monkey helps you see where you are going. Bright and quick-witted, you can see a complicated situation from all sides, including the dark and light, and you weigh the possibilities before acting. You may not always do the predictable thing, though. You communicate well and enjoy having fun, which makes you the center of most social situations. You are a party animal, with lots of friends. Curious about the world and willing to learn from others, you have a special interest in ancient wisdom and the origins of humankind. You would do well as a leader.

If you have become entrenched in a position or point of view, Monkey will appear to remind you to look at things in a different light. It may be that you are developing one area of yourself at the expense of another, or that you are indulging yourself and need to think of others. Remember that the world doesn't revolve around you. Perhaps you need to consider what motivates your choices, so you can be sure to manifest what you really wish for in life. Monkey can help you with insight and inspiration.

Moose: self-esteem

Keywords: **feminine principle, grace, silence, strength**

To almost all North American tribes, the moose has a mystical energy. Some tribes of the northeastern coast of North America associate it with the whale. It is strange and awkward looking, yet majestic and graceful. A solitary animal for most of the year, the moose is at home in every kind of natural environment, including swamps, lakes, open plains, forests, and snowy terrain. It is closely associated with water, which is a symbol of feminine energies, creativity, intuition, and emotion.

If Moose is your totem, you may find that others don't know what to make of you. You can make them smile, but they are often in awe of you. You can explore anywhere, including the depths of your own psyche, and you can blend into any environment. People often forget you are there until you suddenly bring up a surprising new idea or inject new life into a situation. Wise beyond your years, you have a lot to share with others. With Moose as your lifetime guide, you embody a powerful feminine energy. You

are powerfully intuitive and your third eye is open, helping you work with the spirit world.

When Moose crosses your path in a special way, take a moment to appreciate how far you have come in life. You are being shown that you have good reason to feel proud of yourself because you have made steady progress both on the inner planes and in the outer world. Remember also to appreciate those who have helped you. You have learned a lot that is of great value, so now you can encourage and help others. Pay attention to your inner voice, trust your feelings, and refine your sensitivity to yourself and your environment. You might find that a vegetarian diet is suitable for you.

Mouse: scrutiny

Keywords: detail, focus, humility, silence

The ancient Greeks regarded the mouse as sacred to Apollo, the sun god. In ancient Rome, it was a symbol of good luck. The mouse is commonly a witch's familiar, and since it often lives underground, it is associated with the underworld.

With Mouse as your totem, you are a fastidious, well-organized person who pays close attention to detail. Where others may see life as complicated, you are able to see through to simplicity. You like to travel the arcane or hidden ways of knowledge.

If Mouse has twitched its whiskers at you, it may be that in attending to too much detail, you are chewing everything to pieces. Alternatively, you may be neglecting other areas, such as an overall view. Mouse is reminding you to sift through the information and center on what you need to learn. It may be that there is some kind of threat around you. If you have to sign important papers, check them carefully. If you have to deal with new people, study them carefully. Also, study yourself. Remember to stay humble.

Ostrich: practicality

Keywords: power, being grounded

The ostrich is associated with higher knowledge that can be applied in a practical way. It is a fast-moving bird with great strength in its feet, which it can use to kill an enemy if necessary. It is a myth that the ostrich buries its head in the sand when threatened; it simply lowers its head to be less visible.

With Ostrich as your totem, you are a grounded person with an appetite for higher knowledge. Your head is not in the clouds, so you apply knowledge in a practical way. You are not afraid to speak out when you feel it is necessary, but you prefer to go about your daily life without causing trouble.

If Ostrich has caught your attention, it may be that your energies are scattered. Perhaps you are too deeply involved in something and have become vulnerable. Remember that when you attain new knowledge, it takes time to assimilate and digest it before you can use it.

Otter: feminine within

Keywords: adventure, play, joy, perception

In both North America and Africa, medicine women traditionally used otter-skin medicine bags. Known as "water dog" to the Celts, the otter shares some of the symbolism of the dog. The Celtic harp was traditionally kept in a bag made of otter skin. Sacred to the Irish sea-god Manannan, the otter represents deep magic and profound secrets. It is a graceful symbol of the moon and, since it is at home on land and in water, of the feminine energies of creation and emotion. The mother otter cares for her young from birth and teaches them how to swim. Seldom alone, otters spend most of their time eating and playing. They are inquisitive animals, and they will not start a fight.

As a totem, Otter keeps your inner child active. Naturally full of the joy and wonder of life, you like being around other

people and have a great sense of humor. Not a critical person, you don't try to control others and you rarely suffer from envy or jealousy. You work as hard as you play. Honesty is important to you, and you can see below the surface of life to the underlying truth. Otter also helps balance female and male energies. Whether man or woman, you have a strong sense of protectiveness toward your home and children, and you naturally want to help others.

If Otter has made a splash in your life, look around. Perhaps you have become bogged down by negative emotions and Otter is reminding you to take life lightly. Everything has its interesting side. You always have a choice, so call on your goddess within and try something new and creative, simply for the sake of enjoying it. You need to play and to laugh.

Owl: insight

Keywords: **wisdom, clairvoyance, clairaudience, enlightenment, prophecy**

Since ancient times, the owl has been considered the most mysterious of birds. Companion of Athena, Greek goddess of wisdom, and servant of the Roman goddesses Minerva, Sulis, and the crone Hecate, the owl is a symbol of the feminine, the moon and night. In much of the world, it is considered an omen of death. Because it can see in the dark, it is also associated with wisdom and deep contemplation. Owl feathers were used to uncover secrets. In Europe, the owl was considered a witch's familiar, while some North American tribes connected it with healing powers and protection.

Active during both day and night, the owl's sharp sight and acute hearing are associated with clairvoyance and clairaudience.

As your totem, Owl helps you see through masks and illusion and hear what is not being said. You have learned to trust your inner voice concerning the subtleties of other people's motives and actions, so you are not easily deceived. Often you can see right into another person's soul. Strongly individualistic, you prefer working quietly, so you are sensitive to signs and omens, especially when in a new situation. You are aware that your shadow side is a necessary part of the balance of life.

When Owl appears to you in a special way, you may be at a difficult point in your life. Owl is carrying you into the darkness to help you see that both the dark and the light are sacred and that you do not need to be afraid of shadows. Accept yourself, bring your fears to the light, and deal with them sensitively and compassionately. Pay attention to signs, omens, and dream messages.

Panther: mysticism

Keywords: feminine power, rebirth, sensitivity, passion

Throughout world mythology, the panther is a powerful guardian totem. In ancient Egypt, Rome, and Greece, priests often wore a panther skin. In Latin and South America, the panther is a totem that gives the power to do great good or evil. A lunar symbol, rather than the solar of the cougar and lion, it is associated with feminine energies, the dark of the moon, winter and night, darkness, death, and rebirth. Smaller and fiercer than other big cats, the panther is a silent, graceful hunter that can sprint at great speed for a short distance. The female rears her young alone.

If Panther is your totem, you feel yourself to be different from most people. A solitary person, you are happy with your own company, and your friends are usually loners like yourself. Quiet and thoughtful, you do not waste your energy. You cope well under pressure and are adept at multitasking on all levels. A natural inner knowing helps you trust your choices, and you have strong views on how to raise children. Passionate, sensitive, and tactile, you can often read others through touch and are able to persuade others to see as you do, although you are careful not to push them.

When Panther creeps into your vision, it could be that you need protection or support. Perhaps an old wound needs to be healed or a past issue needs to be resolved so you can create space for something new. Panther walks in shadows, so if you fear some part of your shadow side, Panther will help you face it with strength. Panther often shows up during a time of awakening and will help you come into your own power, so you can fulfil your destiny. Don't worry about the future, but be alert for new guidance.

Pig: new life

Keywords: wisdom, truthfulness, fertility

Associated with the goddesses of the moon and the earth, and connected to the underworld, the pig was a fertility symbol to the ancient Egyptians and Greeks. Celtic, Indian, and Greek goddesses were often given the title of "sow." In Celtic myth, a swineherd was an honored position, often a magician or prophet. More recently, piggy banks and lucky charms reflect these attributes.

As your totem, Pig assists you through many trials and tribulations by helping you overcome fears that block your soul's journey. A naturally wise and generous person, you are careful not to let others take advantage of you. You may have an interest in paganism, and you may wish to learn about the three phases of the goddess: maiden, mother, and crone.

When you need guidance concerning new knowledge, or if you are a gullible person, Pig will show up in your life to help you become more discerning. Test the waters and don't believe everything you are told. Pig also reminds you to learn how to say no and to be honest with yourself and others.

Porcupine: trust

Keywords: innocence, faith, humility

A curious, gentle, and good-natured animal, the porcupine uses its quills to defend itself. The quills do not shoot out, but stand up, and are released when they hook into a predator, from which they are almost impossible to remove.

If Porcupine is your totem animal, trust plays a big part in your life. Other people trust you, and you trust yourself, aware that your path in life is part of a greater plan. Able to look after yourself, you enjoy life and can see beyond the weaknesses of others and yourself. You leave a lasting impression wherever you go.

Porcupine shows up in life to help you maintain faith in yourself and to feel comfortable with the way things are unfolding. It may be that you have become impatient about a process, or perhaps pressure or a supposed hurt is making you short-tempered. Porcupine helps you move out of your intellect and into your heart, to reawaken you to the wonder of life. Go with the flow.

Rabbit: sensitivity

Keywords: creativity, optimism, caution, humility

Associated with the moon, the fairy realms, and the underworld, the rabbit is most active at dawn and dusk—the "in-between times." In *Alice's Adventures in Wonderland* by Lewis Carroll, it is a white rabbit that Alice follows down a hole under a tree at the beginning of her great adventure. One of the most common prey animals, the rabbit has long been a symbol for fertility and sexuality throughout the world. While Westerners see the rabbit as weak, in many Asian cultures it is seen as a clever survivor who can use its strong teeth for defense. One can say that in many areas of the world the rabbit is more like Bugs Bunny than a soft, weak loser.

With Rabbit as your totem, you are a sensitive and flexible person, ready to change as the situation changes. You may appear to progress in leaps and jumps, but in fact you are optimizing your creativity and your fertility of mind, heart, and body. Rabbit also helps you attune to the phases of the moon, so you are aware

of its influence on yourself and your endeavors, and you plan accordingly. Well organized, you do not announce your moves but keep your head down so that others cannot take advantage of you. Loving, artistic, and sensitive, you are probably a vegetarian. You also know how important it is to have still and quiet times.

Rabbit can show up in your life when you are faced with a new and perhaps worrying situation or if you feel blocked. Rabbit will help you uncover any negative feelings. Meditate to release them, so that you are ready to move quickly.

Ram: regeneration

Keywords: power, creativity, generosity

In ancient Egypt, Khnum, the god of creation, and Amun, the god of air and fertility, were depicted with a ram's head. Throughout Asia and Africa, the sacrificial ram played a major part in fertility rites. The ram's association with fire, strength, and immortality gave rise to the tale of the quest for the Golden Fleece, a spiritual treasure. The ram's horn is a spiral, which is a symbol of creativity, rebirth, and expansion. A battering ram symbolizes great physical strength.

If Ram is your totem, you are a physically and mentally active person. You love life and live it to the full, and you love adventure. You seek knowledge and have a vivid imagination. Your emotions are powerful, you are sensitive and sometimes stubborn, but you have a great inner strength that carries you through many of life's challenges. Ram teaches you trust in yourself; you will always land on your feet.

Ram appears in your life when you are ready to start something new, helping you with inspiration and encouraging you to put your head down and make things happen. It is time to develop your personal power. Be aware of how you use it, and keep it under control so you don't dominate others.

Rat: success

Keywords: activity, foresight, wealth

Throughout Asia, the rat is a symbol of good luck. In ancient Egypt, it was considered sacred. When rats leave a house or ship, it is seen as a sign of misfortune. A very intelligent, courageous, and sociable animal, the rat is highly adaptable and can survive in almost any environment.

If your totem is Rat, you are an intelligent person, shrewd in your dealings with others. You like to be active, and you can get the best out of most situations because you plan ahead. Success is important to you. You enjoy a busy social life and you fit easily into different environments. When challenged, you readily defend yourself.

Rat appears in your life to help you reconnect to your innate intuitive ability. Perhaps you have been sitting around instead of getting on with manifesting your dreams and desires, or you are driving yourself too hard, making yourself uptight, and you need to take a break. You may already have noticed things that are going wrong. It's also possible that Rat is telling you that you are sticking

your nose where it is not wanted. Examine your motives; be honest with yourself and with others.

Raven: magic

Keywords: **intelligence, creativity, ingenuity, clairvoyance, manifestation**

Widely respected because of its intelligence, and considered a good omen in many cultures, the raven is connected to the sun. In ancient Greece, it was sacred to Apollo. Ancient Romans believed that the call of the raven, "cras," which means "tomorrow" in Latin, represented hope. In Norse myth, two ravens called Hugin (mind) and Munnin (memory) were associated with Odin. A raven was released from Noah's ark as the flood receded, so it is a symbol of clear-sightedness. Among the tribes of the Pacific Northwest, it was a raven that set the world in order. The Celts considered

the raven very sacred. A bird of prophecy, it was also connected to war. Ravens have occupied the Tower of London for centuries, and legend has it that the British kingdom will fall should the ravens ever depart. The negative view of the raven is fairly recent, apparently only since the development of agriculture, and is a view that exists solely in Europe. Extremely intelligent, the raven uses tools. It is playful, and it can even learn to speak. Swift and cautious, it has no fear of other birds.

One of the most powerful totems, Raven guides the development of consciousness. If Raven is your totem, you are already a long way on a spiritual path. You meditate conscientiously, have a strong will, and understand the power of thought and intention, so you can manifest what you want to achieve with ease. You may be a healer or have an interest in ancient hidden knowledge. A very creative person, you seem to come up with ideas and inspiration out of the blue. Confident and adaptable, you are cautious in new situations. Time alone is important to you, but you are lively among company. You connect well with all creatures.

If Raven has called to you, then pay attention, because a very powerful time is just ahead. You have been learning a great deal, and you are probably already committed to a regular practice of meditation and prayer. Because of your spiritual progress, a change in consciousness or a new reality is coming. If fear holds you back, Raven will guide you into your shadow side to face it so it can be transmuted. Raven will help you understand how to use your considerable energy in a positive way. Acknowledge the wonder and magic of life with love and humility.

Rhinoceros: discrimination

Keywords: ancient wisdom, self-knowledge

Found in Africa and Asia, the rhinoceros is descended from the pre-historic era of mammoths and sabre-toothed tigers. It lives in small family groups or alone. It is considered extremely dangerous, as it can defend itself very well when disturbed.

With Rhino as your totem, you do not easily become unbalanced when faced with challenging events or difficult people, because you trust in your intuition and are able to keep things in perspective. You have hidden depths, and you are interested in spirituality and ancient wisdom; you put into practice what you are learning. You may be quite shy and solitary, preferring not to draw attention to yourself.

Rhino comes into your vision to help you learn to pay attention to your inner voice. It also helps you look deeper into life and to study and understand the past. Only by knowing where we have been can we understand where we are going.

Robin: new growth

Keywords: courage, perspective, strength

Common throughout North America and Europe, the robin is noted for its courage. In European lore, it is associated with the winter solstice, Robin Hood, and the tradition of the Yule log, which, when burned, sends the spirit of the year up the chimney. The spirit that is seen flying away is symbolized as a robin. It is still the custom to make a wish for good luck when seeing the first robin of the year. In Norse myth, the robin is sacred to Thor, the god of thunder and lightning.

As your totem, Robin helps your spirit be strong. Even in the most difficult situations, you are aware that there is light at the end of the tunnel, which gives you the strength and courage to get through the darkest times. You are not attached to material things or to your ideas and opinions, so you can let go of them to make space for the new.

If Robin has come to you in a special way, it may be to help you let go of something you have outgrown—maybe an opinion that is holding you back or material goods that you worry too much about. Perhaps you need to establish boundaries. It may seem like you are being called to sacrifice something, but whatever it is, take heart, because letting go of something will allow new growth into your life.

Salmon: wisdom

Keywords: ancestral knowledge, perseverance, willpower, serenity, healing

Especially sacred to the Druids and Celts, the salmon was seen as the store of ancient wisdom, and it was believed that eating it granted second sight. It was also associated with healing. Today, fish oil is known to nourish the brain. As the salmon lives in both freshwater and salt water, it is linked to the feminine and to emotions, dreams, and the imagination. Eating fish on Friday, the day of the goddess, is a pre-Christian tradition.

With Salmon as your totem, you love to explore knowledge about the origins of life. Focused on your spiritual path, you are happy to take a leap into the unknown for the sake of ancient knowledge. Enthusiastic and quietly confident, you have the strength and stamina to overcome any kind of obstacle. People are often drawn to you because of your charm and strength. Dreams are important to you, and you may be drawn to work as a healer.

Salmon appears to you to help you through a time of spiritual development. Study the past, as it will help you with what is coming next. Perhaps you are in need of healing or creative inspiration or you are going through an emotional time and feel lost. Salmon can assist you in sharpening your perception and strengthening your will, so that you know when to be still and when to act.

Seal: imagination

Keywords: creativity, balance, play

Associated with the ocean and the land, the seal moves most easily and gracefully in the watery realms, which are linked with emotion, imagination, and creativity. The seal has a playful side to its nature.

If Seal is your totem, you may be an artist, musician, or writer. Certainly, you are very creative and you have a vivid imagination, and it is important to you that your ideas and dreams come to fruition. Seal helps keep you grounded while you are in this process. You have an active social life, and you are fun to be with. You like to be near water.

If Seal has made a splash in your life, it is to help you with a new creative task or to help you cope with a time of change. You may be holding yourself back because you worry about what others might think or say. Alternatively, you may feel blocked in some way. Whatever the situation, Seal is giving your imagination a push. Make note of your dreams at this time. It may be that you have been trying too hard and need to find balance, so Seal is telling you it is fine to take time out to have some fun.

Snake: transmutation

Keywords: rebirth, regeneration, healing, clairsentience

Long before it became a symbol of evil among Christian societies, from ancient times the snake was linked to the secrets of life, death, and rebirth. It is also associated with insight, wisdom, guardianship and protection, prophecy, and divination. The image of a snake swallowing its own tail (the ouroboros) is a symbol of this eternal cycle. Due to its sinuous movement, the snake is a symbol of water, and it is associated with sacred wells and healing. The caduceus, with two intertwined snakes, is an ancient symbol of healing and medicine that is still used today. In yoga, the kundalini is seen as a serpent fire that sits at the base of the spine

and rises through practice and preparation to activate new levels of awareness and healing. Snake poison is used in shamanic traditions throughout the world to induce trance states.

It is a rare person who has Snake as a totem. Already far along the spiritual path, highly developed on all levels, strong-willed, vibrant, and sensitive to all kinds of energies, you are a balanced person who understands oneness. Perhaps you have had a near-death experience that Snake has helped you put to good use. Certainly, you are aware that all experience, both positive and negative, has great value. Your sense of smell may be especially sensitive; this most refined of the senses is linked to higher spiritual development. You like to learn about the spiritual practices of indigenous groups. You want to understand ancient knowledge and metaphysical and esoteric subjects, and you easily assimilate what you learn. Able to sense or see auras, you can perceive imbalance in others. You may be a healer or even a spiritual leader, as you have a deep desire to bring about positive transformation in the world.

If Snake has crossed your path, it is time to shed an old idea, opinion, habit, or even relationship. A new cycle is about to begin in some area of your life, so you may experience a change of consciousness or a major life change. You need help to face something that is holding you back. Letting go is not easy, but you need to make space for new issues. Perhaps you have been ill or you feel threatened or feel that you lack strength. Snake is reminding you that you generate your own fear. Anything scary or uncomfortable can be transformed with the right approach and mental attitude. Positive thought is the source of every event. Be aware of thought, and then control what it does by the words you use.

Spider: weaving of destiny

Keywords: creativity, wisdom, illusion, balance

Worldwide, the spider is considered to be a cosmic creator, weaver of the fabric of the world. Both lunar and solar, it is linked to the goddesses of fate who spin and weave, such as Arachne in ancient Greece. The fragile web represents the veil of material illusion that hides the supreme reality, and its spiral form is a traditional representation of creative development. Among North American tribes, the spider is Grandmother, the teacher of language and writing, based on the geometric pattern in the web. In Africa, the

Lord Spider, Anansi, is seen as a hero-trickster. Having eight legs and a body shaped in the figure of an eight, the spider is the symbol of infinity, and associated with unlimited possibilities.

Although small, Spider is a powerful totem. With Spider as your guide, you are a balanced person, strong yet gentle, wise, and well able to express your creativity. You are aware that everything you think, feel, say, or do in the present is not only shaping your future but also reverberating everywhere, like ripples from a pebble thrown into a pond. You perceive the way in which the past and present lead toward the future, and you know that everything is connected to and dependent on everything else, including all life on earth, as well as the stars and the planets and the universe. Yet as the weaver at the center of your own reality, you also appreciate that there is only one journey in life, and that is your own.

If Spider has dropped into your vision, you are being helped to express your creativity. Spider's guidance will help you stay focused as you move toward the goal of bringing your ideas and dreams into manifestation. Just as Spider will build its web repeatedly until it is done properly, you, too, must never give up. Writing a journal may be helpful. Spider is also reminding you to honor the balance between male and female and to understand the way that the past influences the present and the future. It may be that you are too closely involved in a situation and cannot see your way through it, or that you are too wrapped up in yourself. Whatever the situation, you can change your reality as you wish.

Squirrel: preparation

Keywords: energetic activity, perseverance, discovery

In Teutonic and Norse myth, the squirrel lived in the World Ash Tree, Yggdrasil, which was the mythical tree of life. The squirrel is the messenger between the snake at the bottom of the tree and the eagle at the top. It was sacred to Thor, god of fire and thunder.

With Squirrel as your totem, you are an organized person. Naturally efficient, you learn from experience rather than through study, and you often have new ideas. You trust in the abundance of life, yet like to plan ahead so you are prepared for any eventuality. Over the years, Squirrel has assisted you in gathering personal power, which you use wisely.

When Squirrel makes a remarkable appearance in your life, a very active time is just ahead of you. Squirrel is reminding you not to rush around and waste your energy, but to plan and work steadily toward your goals. Don't chatter about what you are doing to others, as this may dissipate your energy. Remember not to be caught up in self-importance; take time out to relax and have fun. If you fear being short of money, let intuition rather than fear act as your guide, and trust that with a bit of effort on your part, you will get the help you need. Squirrel guides you to balance getting with giving. If you have too much "stuff," share or recycle some of it in some way.

Swan: grace

Keywords: inner beauty, strength, intuition, mystery, partnership, song

Worldwide, a mass of myth, tradition, and poetry has gathered around the swan. An ancient totem, both solar and lunar, the swan is a symbol of both masculine and feminine, and mystery and holiness. King of the water birds, to the Celts it represented the angelic realms, and its skin and feathers traditionally made up the cloak of Celtic poets. Throughout northern Europe, it was taboo to kill a swan. The swan mates for life. It is a powerful bird that can kill with a blow of its wing.

If Swan is your totem, you have an inner beauty that is readily brought out into the world. Sensitive to your own emotions and those of others, you can see what lies behind a word or action and perceive the true spirit of a person. Trusting in your inner sight and power, you glide through change smoothly and gracefully. You may be a poet, a dreamer, or a mystic, and you have a childlike innocence that covers a silent form of strength. Being alone in nature is important to you, as is fidelity. In partnership, you are not likely to be satisfied with anyone who is less than a "twin flame."

Swan appears in your life to bring you the awareness that no matter how things seem on the surface, you have inner beauty and power. Let go of your ego so that higher forces can guide you. Spend some time alone by water, touching the earth and paddling. Reflect on your development. You are being called to a new level of awareness, and your intuitive abilities are being deepened. Remember that there is rhythm and harmony in the universe and there is a greater plan. When you accept that you are beautiful and learn to love yourself, then your true mate can appear.

Tiger: strength

Keywords: confidence, vitality, focus, patience, beauty, healing, passion

Terrifying yet fascinating, noble "lord of the jungle," the tiger is honored in mythology throughout Asia. In China, it is a mystical symbol of protective strength and is linked to healing. To Buddhists, the tiger represents spiritual struggle and maintaining an inner light through a dark and difficult time. A nocturnal and solitary creature, the tiger can travel immense distances in search of prey. Hunting slowly and silently, it will make its move suddenly and accurately. It is an excellent swimmer, and the mother tiger is devoted to her young.

With Tiger as your totem, you are a confident person with great focus and patience. You have the ability to sense the most beneficial time to act. You are so tranquil that you often surprise people; they have little idea how watchful and prepared you are. Privacy is essential to you, and you work quietly, not broadcasting your many abilities. Some of your best work is done alone and at night. Charismatic, sensitive, and tactile, you may be involved in the healing arts. Since Tiger teaches clairvoyance and clairaudience, over time, with practice and patience, you learn to see into realms other than the mundane.

When Tiger appears, a new adventure is ahead. Tiger is at hand to assist you with self-control, being observant, and saving your energy until it is the right time to act. You may be called to take on a leadership role, and you need the extra strength and courage that Tiger can help provide. Change can be a challenge, but Tiger will empower you to move through it smoothly and with dignity.

Toad: good fortune

Keywords: sensitivity, creativity, non-judgment, wealth

Throughout the world, the toad is linked to water, darkness, and the moon. In China, it is a symbol of fertility and wealth. In the West, it is said to be a guardian of treasure, and it also helps when someone is giving birth. Associated by the Celts with the underworld, the earth goddess, and healing, the toad is said to have a precious stone in its head.

Whether you are male or female, if Toad is your totem, you are strongly connected to your feminine side. Able to draw on powerful inner resources, you are not swayed by bad luck. You have strength and patience that will carry you through the darkest of times, because you know that the most difficult lessons carry the most valuable teachings. Sensitive to vibration, you do not judge by appearances, and you see people as they truly are, no matter what might be reflected on the surface. Dreams feature strongly in your life.

When Toad shows up in your life in a special way, prepare yourself for a fertile time. Your dreams may become especially vivid. Keep a notebook by your bed so you can record them as soon as you wake. Look within to see whether you are harboring any prejudices or negative judgments about yourself, others, or a situation. Things are often not as they appear on the surface. Toad will help you discern the beauty within.

Turtle: mother energy

Keywords: ancient knowledge, discrimination, meditation, protection

One of the most ancient of symbols throughout the world, the turtle is seen to represent the planet. Its shell is curved like the heavens, rising over the flat plane of its body, the earth. Native American legends tell how the first land grew on the turtle's back, becoming the whole earth. In ancient China, turtle shells were used for divination. Linked to lunar cycles and female energy, the turtle moves between water and land, reflecting the subtle energies of both realms.

You are an old soul, if Turtle is your totem. Well-grounded, you have a great respect for the earth and its natural rhythms. Aware of the need to withdraw from the world from time to time, you

meditate regularly. Always working at a calm and measured pace, you appreciate and honor your creativity, both its source in spirit and its manifestation in the material. Sensitive and compassionate, you listen well and can read between the lines. Turtle also helps you know how to protect yourself from negative energies and too high a level of emotional involvement.

If Turtle appears in your life or your dreams, it may be that you have become too caught up in today's fast-moving world. Perhaps you feel like you never have enough time for all the things you wish or need to do. Turtle is calling you to stop for a while and sit alone and in silence, to meditate, go within until you see how the flow is going and can determine your place in it. Think before you act because speed is not the best way to accomplish things. When you move at a measured pace, your senses become heightened, physically and spiritually. It may be that Turtle is telling you to ground yourself or that you simply need to rest and sit in the sun for a while. If things are difficult, remember that Turtle carries protective energy.

Vulture: renewal

Keywords: cleansing, efficiency, mysticism

Royal bird of the Maya, the vulture is seen throughout the world as the cleanser who ensures the endless cycle of renewal. It is associated with fertility and spiritual and material wealth in Africa and Asia and with the protection of the pharaoh in ancient Egypt. In Greco-Roman times, the vulture was considered a bird of augury.

As your totem, Vulture helps you use your energy efficiently and to recycle things that others throw away. You get on with your life in a quiet way because you don't care to make a fuss. One of your main areas of interest is mysticism. Blessed with keen insight and discrimination, you are likely to develop visionary qualities as you mature.

Vulture appears when you need to take a good look at your life because something is not quite right about it. Vulture can help you pick over which projects or things, or perhaps people, need to be cleared away, to allow for progress, change, or something new.

Weasel: secrecy

Keywords: **watchfulness, stealth, persistence**

In the Celtic tradition, the weasel is associated with the warrior, because while being graceful and agile, it is a fierce little animal that has an extraordinary amount of energy. A symbol of moral purity, the white fur of the ermine, or stoat (a close relative of the weasel), is traditionally used as trim on the robes of royalty, priests, and academics.

A challenging totem, Weasel inspires you to be energetic and courageous. Trusting in your ability to get out of difficult situations, you are ready to try anything. It is important to you to see projects through to completion. You like to be alone, but since you are observant and very quiet when you are in a group, people tend to forget that you are there, enabling you to learn a lot without being noticed. This might not always endear you to others, as you can see hidden strengths and weaknesses and also understand what is really going on. You are not easily fooled. You are very protective of your family.

Weasel turns up to help you deal with other people. If you are quiet and watchful, with Weasel's assistance you will swiftly learn to trust your instincts about whom you can trust or whether you should move forward alone. It might be best not to talk about what you have found out. Silence does not mean that you are weak; it is simply wise not to gossip. Just go about your creative pursuits quietly so that no energy is wasted. Be honest with yourself and others, and use what you learn for the good of all.

Whale: inner depths

Keywords: **ancient knowledge, wisdom, initiation, resurrection, clairaudience**

In many cultures, the whale plays a part in initiation myths, because passing through the belly of the whale represents the time of darkness between two states of being. In some traditions, the whale is the bearer of the cosmos, or a symbol of buried treasure. It is said to carry the history of the planet. As it is a mammal that lives in the ocean and breathes air, the whale represents the balanced subtle energies of these two realms.

Whale is the totem of an old soul with a lifelong interest in ancient knowledge. Although you are a quiet, reflective person, when you choose to speak up, you surprise others with your knowledge and wisdom about universal truths and principles. As you mature, you often have cosmic insights that you may joke seem to "come from the top of your head," while quietly appreciating the power of an open crown chakra. With Whale as your guide, you have learned the value of yogic breathing and meditation. You are calm and steady, and you can go deeply into yourself or into altered states of consciousness quite easily. You may have developed a degree of telepathy and clairaudience. Singing and chanting are important to you, and you use both for healing and balance. A creative person, with Whale's guidance you have the ability to express your full potential.

If Whale has appeared to you in a special manner, it is to remind you not to be afraid of your light and to appreciate your creative

energy and let it shine in the world. You have a tendency to get lost in what you are doing. Remember to appreciate the world around you. If you need to clear negative energy and tension from your body, imitate the Whale by blowing air out of your body while thrusting your hands away from your solar plexus chakra. Learn about chanting, as this is another way to manifest spirituality in your life. Along with drumming, these are time-honored ways to get in touch with ancient memories at a cellular level. All that you need is within you.

Wolf: teacher and pathfinder

Keywords: intelligence, affection, discrimination, compassion

Traditionally epitomizing the wild spirit in Europe, since medieval times the wolf has been one of the most misunderstood and maligned of all wild creatures. However, North Americans tribes, like many other indigenous peoples, traditionally called the wolf "brother" for the profound teachings it carried for humans. Some traditions believe that the wolf is represented by Sirius, the Dog Star, which they consider to be the home of the ancients. Powerful and highly intelligent, wolves are social creatures. Each one has a special place and role in the pack, and all cooperate to care for the young. They communicate using expressive body language and sounds that change from puppyhood through adolescence to adulthood. When the moon is full, their songs seem dedicated to the heavens. A wolf never wastes anything, and it goes out of its way to avoid trouble.

If Wolf is your totem, the teacher in you is empowered to come out. Using expressive body language, you passionately share your knowledge about things of the heart and soul by writing or speaking, by using examples and telling stories. Emotional and affectionate, you have a strong sense of family and community, and also of yourself, so finding balance between family life and individual freedom is important to you. You do not like waste. Wolf howls at the moon, and this is a symbol of psychic energy; for you, this represents the new ideas that are just below the surface of your consciousness. For these to manifest, you sometimes need to seek out high or lonely places to meditate. Although you avoid confrontation, you can fight if you need to.

When Wolf appears in your life, it is time not to rely on gurus or outer teachers but instead to learn to trust your inner voice and develop your intuition. Seek within yourself for answers. Learning discrimination will help you avoid inappropriate action. As a guide to new knowledge, Wolf can help you step out onto a new path or find balance in your life. True freedom requires self-discipline and personal responsibility.

Wren: healing power of nature

Keywords: practicality, resourcefulness, courage, rebirth

Sacred to the Druids, in Celtic tradition the wren was connected to Bran, god of death and resurrection. Its song was used for divination. It was considered unlucky to kill a wren, except ritually at the winter solstice. In some cultural myths, the wren was thought to have brought fire to humankind. Legend has it that the bird that flew the highest was to become king of the birds. Tiny but bold, the wren hid itself among the feathers on the back of the eagle, and when the eagle could go no higher, the wren flew that little bit farther, earning itself the title.

As your totem, Wren helps you be a practical person, knowing your strengths and how best to use them. You speak up when you need to, and others pay attention when you do. Interested in arcane teachings and forgotten traditions, you like to spend time in ancient woodlands or forests and by sacred wells and springs. Watching animals is fascinating to you, and you have an interest in healing herbs. You may be a keen gardener.

If Wren has caught your attention, it may be in order to boost your confidence. Perhaps you have a budding interest in learning about the healing power of nature or protecting the environment. Wren will guide you in these areas and help you find the courage to speak up about them. Find a tranquil spot in nature that somehow resonates with you, and spend time there in silence. Let the earth speak to you.

Conclusion

I have learned that from time to time, a new totem animal will appear in a special way that is beyond mere chance or coincidence. This seems to happen when something new or different is about to occur or when something new is already manifesting in my life. Even though I don't yet know what's about to happen, the totem animal knows that I will soon need a specific type of guidance that only this particular creature can give. Be constantly alive to the appearance of animals that are local to your area, whether they are wild or domesticated.

You may see a fox slinking along an alleyway or among the undergrowth; then it stops still and, instead of racing swiftly for cover, looks directly at you for a long, breathless moment. At last, it leisurely walks away, leaving you with the feeling that something unusual has happened. The fox has clearly come to give you a message.

Suppose you almost trip over a snake basking on your doorstep as you leave your house. You might not be sure of the symbolism of the snake, so you will need to look it up. The first idea that pops into your head might be correct, but remember that we have also been subject to conditioning, and there is perhaps no better example of this than the snake!

Perhaps you are feeling agitated and you ask your totem animal for help before you fall asleep at night. In the early morning, the cooing of a dove on your windowsill wakes you. Looking up the meaning of the dove, and you will see it has come to remind you to choose serenity of mind.

Alternatively, you may ask your totem animal for help and find an image of an elephant showing up in your life—someone gives you a picture of an elephant or you see elephants on the television. Maybe the elephant is bringing you a message about determination and resolve.

An animal might show up in an unusual place or make a sound that seems odd or that specifically catches your attention. It might show itself persistently—classically three times. For example, a crow recently came into my life in a special way, and it was clearly directing me even though I didn't have any idea that I was in need of guidance. First of all, while I was on my way to a special meeting, four crows appeared in the distance, and they were acting in such an unusual manner that I thought I was seeing eagles rather than crows. I understood that this strange behavior might be carrying a message. I soon found myself being guided by the croaking of a crow to a special place, and a short while later, I found a black feather on the ground. When I studied the essence of the crow, I understood how to deal with some new people I had to

meet concerning some work that is very important to me. Crow appeared to give me help in that specific area.

The new totem animal may manifest as a cloud shape. It may come to you in a dream or during meditation. It might even be something as simple as a picture in a book that catches your attention. In any of these circumstances, be aware that a message is being given to you.

White feathers are universally famous for appearing on the ground or floating down through the air in front of you at a time when you are worried about something. Some people say that an eagle has just passed over, while others say that it is an angel. Whatever your belief, if you see this sign, be reassured that everything is unfolding as it should and that you should give your concern over to your Creator.

I wish you well on your journey.

Index of Totem Animals

Ant: self-sacrifice   42

Badger: willpower   42

Bat: initiation   44

Bear: self-sufficiency   45

Beaver: achievement   46

Bee: creativity and mystery   47

Bison: spiritual abundance   48

Blackbird: new beginning   49

Boar: honor   50

Bull: determination   51

Butterfly: transformation   52

Cat: mystery   54

Cougar: leadership   55

Coyote: paradox   56

Crane: regeneration   58

Crow: sacred law   59

Deer: gentleness   60

Dog: loyalty   61

Dolphin: compassion   62

Dove: serenity   64

Dragonfly: power of light   65

Eagle: spirit   66

Elephant: resolve   67

Elk: stamina   69

Fox: guile   70

Frog: renewal   71

Giraffe: foresight   72

Goat: perspective   73

Grasshopper: extraordinary leaps forward   74

Hare: creativity   75

Hawk/falcon): spiritual perception   76

Hedgehog: self-knowledge   78

Heron: hidden wisdom   79

Horse: mobility   80

Kangaroo: balance   81

Kingfisher: prosperity   82

Lion: dignity   83

Lizard: ancient knowledge   84

Magpie: metaphysical knowledge   85

Monkey: agility   86

Moose: self-esteem   88

Mouse: scrutiny   90

Ostrich: practicality   91

Otter: feminine within   92

Owl: insight   93

Panther: mysticism   95

Pig: new life   97

Porcupine: trust   98

Rabbit: sensitivity   98

Ram: regeneration   100

Rat: success   101

Raven: magic   102

Rhinoceros: discrimination   104

Robin: new growth   105

Salmon: wisdom   106

Seal: imagination   107

Snake: transmutation   108

Spider: weaving of destiny   110

Squirrel: preparation   111

Swan: grace   113

Tiger: strength   114

Toad: good fortune   116

Turtle: mother energy   117

Vulture: renewal   118

Weasel: secrecy   119

Whale: inner depths   120

Wolf: teacher and pathfinder   122

Wren: healing power of nature   124

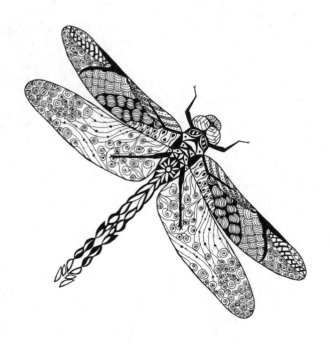

About the Author

Celia Gunn is a Northumbrian writer and novelist who has lived in Israel and Canada, working in publishing and education. Closely involved in the renascence of the Sinixt First Nation in British Columbia, she is the author of a memoir *A Twist in Coyote's Tale*, which has been adapted into a film entitled *The Sinixt: Bringing Home the Bones*. She continues to be involved with the Sinixt in their struggle for full representation.

When not planning and researching her writing, Celia can most often be found tending her beautiful woodland chakra garden.